Published by Action Duchenne February 2009

www.actionduchenne.org

ISBN 978-0-9561892-0-2

This book includes references to nuts and recipes including nuts, nut derivatives and nut oils. Avoid if you have a known allergic reaction to nuts, nut derivatives and nut oils. Pregnant and nursing mothers, invalids, the elderly, children and babies may be potentially vulnerable to nut allergies and should therefore avoid nuts, nut derivatives and nut oils.

The Caledonian Kitchen

Compiled by
Julie & Kenny Munro

Foreword by
Kaye Adams

Contents

F220M

Foreword

By Kaye Adams

Thank you so much for buying this recipe book and giving hope to all the boys and young men living with Duchenne Muscular Dystrophy in the UK.

It's an incredibly distressing and progressive genetic disorder which gradually causes sufferers to lose the ability to do things like walk, sit upright, breathe easily, and move their arms and hands. Most sufferers will be using a wheel-chair by the time they are eight or ten and the condition is, invariably, life-limiting.

On average two boys are born in the UK every week with Duchenne and around 100 young lives are lost to the condition each year.

But, on the positive side, there are very exciting developments in the search for a cure for Duchenne Muscular Dystrophy.

This is by no means a lost cause and, with your help, we have a realistic chance of transforming the lives of DMD children and their families.

Kaye Adams

A Message From Action Duchenne

By Nick Catlin, CEO and founder member of Action Duchenne

For too long Duchenne Muscular Dystrophy has been a forgotten condition. Many families, like mine, had never heard of Duchenne and then suddenly one day you find yourself sitting in a clinician's room numb with shock as you are told your lovely little boy will be paralysed by early teens and will die in late teens early twenties from heart or respiratory failure. We were offered little hope when our lovely Saul was diagnosed with this genetic severe muscle wasting disease. In fact we were told to go and enjoy what was left of our lives together. But how do you do that when you are living every day with this death sentence?

For Janet and I the answer was to get out and fight back against Duchenne. We found some other families via the internet and with inspiration from the wonderful Pat Furlong in the USA we launched a new Charity now called Action Duchenne. Our aim then and now is to find the new drugs and gene therapies to cure this disease. We are still determined to save this generation of young people from the hopeless diagnosis that we were given.

Now Action Duchenne has funded a number of exciting research projects and we are proud to be part of the consortium that is running the first in man clinical trials for a gene therapy for Duchenne in the UK. We have funded new drug discovery projects and we are working with a team to find out if we can use stem cells to treat Duchenne.

To my delight, I attended a clinic at Great Ormond Street the other day to find two families waiting for pre medical assessments so that they could be part of two new trials for the Duchenne drug PTC124 and the MDEX exon skipping gene therapy project. It is only a small step towards our search for a cure but I felt at least there was hope in all our hearts that their sons were on the road to better treatments.

But so much more has to be done. This wonderful book and project started by Julie and Kenny Munro is yet another inspiring contribution to our campaign to cure Duchenne. Thank you for buying the book as all funds will go directly to our mission to fund further research and see an end to this disease. Please pass on the message, join us on our website **www.actionduchenne.org** and sell more copies to friends and family – Saul and I are off to get cooking!

Acknowledgements

Our warm and heartfelt thanks to everyone who has made this book possible, the support we have received has been simply overwhelming.

Firstly, we would like to thank the forty Scottish celebrities and prominent figures who have taken the time to contribute their favourite recipe to this cause. Special thanks go to Kaye Adams, Eileen McCallum, Rob Maclean and also David Reid.

This project would not have proceeded without the generous donations from the award winning Scottish restaurants who contributed so much towards the design and printing costs. Not only did they make a significant financial contribution but also spent a lot of their precious time preparing their recipes and photographs.

To all our family, friends and the supporters of the charity whose donations have also made a huge contribution towards the publication of the book. Their generosity has surpassed all expectations.

The book has been designed to the highest quality by the design team at Touchpaper Design who have given up so much of their invaluable time. Thanks must also go to David Robertson of www.scot-image.co.uk who provided the wonderful photographs of Scotland.

Many thanks to the sponsors, Charles Macleod Butchers, Braehead Foods, The Island Cheese Company, Norco Energy and Röchling Engineering Plastics who have lent their support.

And finally, thank you so much to all of you who have bought this book. In doing so you are directly funding ongoing and future research into this cruel condition.

Our son, Ross, pictured below, is presently participating in a clinical trial for an investigational drug, PTC124, which has been developed in the U.S.A. It is hoped that the drug will benefit 13% of Duchenne sufferers. The development of this drug was made possible by the fundraising efforts of American parents to whom we are indebted. Hopefully, the funds now raised in the U.K. can also lead to new drug discoveries and treatments for all the people suffering from Duchenne Muscular Dystrophy.

Hope you enjoy the book. If you would like more books, you can visit our website at **http://www.thecaledoniankitchen.co.uk** to find out how to obtain them.

Julie and Kenny Munro
Clarkston, Glasgow

February 2009

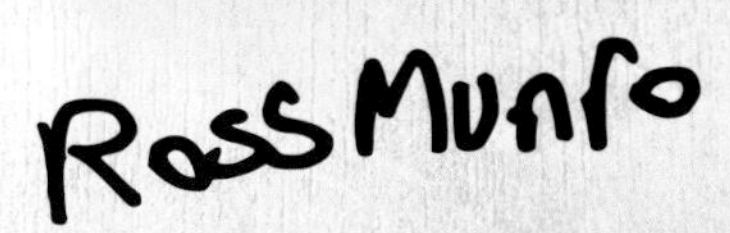

Celebrities

Risotto With Prawn, Lemon, Spring Onion and Basil

by Kaye Adams

INGREDIENTS

Olive oil

1/2 onion, finely chopped

1 clove of garlic, peeled and finely chopped

150g risotto rice

75ml white wine

750ml warm light vegetable stock

A bunch of spring onions, thinly sliced

150g cooked peeled prawns

3 tablespoons low-fat crème fraîche

A squeeze of lemon

1/2 bunch of basil, chopped

Salt and freshly ground black pepper

Kaye Adams is a Television Presenter

METHOD

Heat up a splash of oil and gently fry the onion and garlic until translucent. Add the rice and continue frying for two minutes. Add the wine and continue stirring until the wine is absorbed.

Now start to add the stock, ladle by ladle, stirring until the stock is absorbed between each spoonful.

Give the risotto lots of tender loving care, by stirring regularly, and the creamy starch will come out of each grain. Continue like this for 10 to 15 minutes.

Add the spring onion to the risotto, continue cooking for five minutes and then add the prawns and crème fraîche.

Now this is the important point. You need the rice to be al dente, which means firm-to-bite (not soft and overcooked), so keep tasting it until it is time to take it off the heat (it will probably need another five minutes).

Add a squeeze of lemon and stir through the basil. Check the seasoning and then, for the final touch, grate some lemon zest over the top.

Kaye Adams

Chargrilled Chicken Breast, Rocket and Pine Nut Salad with a Sundried Tomato Dressing

by Duncan Bannatyne

INGREDIENTS

1 chicken breast

1 bunch rocket

4oz pine nuts

4oz sundried tomatoes

2tsp white wine vinegar

olive oil

METHOD

Cook chicken on char grill for 5 mins each side then place in oven for further 10 mins.

Toast the pine nuts under the grill for 2 mins.

Place the sundried tomatoes in water for 5 mins then drain.

Place the sundried tomatoes in a food processor with the white wine vinegar, gradually add olive oil and blend into sauce consistency.

Place the rocket then pine nuts on plate, lay the chicken breast on top and drizzle the dressing around.

Duncan Bannatyne OBE is an Entrepreneur and star of BBC's Dragons' Den

Pasta Bresaola

by Scott Booth

INGREDIENTS

Serves: 4

Pasta

Bresaola (Pulled apart unevenly)

Garlic (4-5 cloves or to choice)

2 Onions, one white one red (Large)

4 Spring onions

A Baby Leek (Chopped)

Parmesan (Grated) small cup and (Shavings) small cup.

Fresh Pesto (1 tub green, 1 tub red…Marks & Spencer!)

Basil (Plenty and finely chopped)

Capers (Roughly chopped)

White wine (Half glass)

Olive oil

Extra Virgin Olive oil

Salt

Freshly ground black pepper

Eight Basil Leaves and several capers (For decoration)

Scott Booth is a former Scottish International Footballer and is now a Football Commentator

METHOD

Cook the pasta in a large pan (plenty water) with a chicken stock cube and a splash of oil. When 'al dente' (firm, not soggy!) turn off the heat, drain and return to the pan. Mix a small splash of olive oil through and put the lid on to keep warm.

Finely chop the onion and slice the garlic. Add 3tbsp of oil to the pan on medium heat and once the oil is hot, throw in the onions and stir gently. After a few minutes add the garlic.

When the garlic has a slight golden tinge, turn the heat up a bit and add the wine. When the wine is almost bubbled away, reduce the heat again adding the capers, spring onion and Bresaola pieces. Stir through for a minute.

Add the mixture from the frying pan to the pasta and stir in well. Heat the pasta extremely gently again adding all the pesto, finely chopped basil and a splash of extra virgin olive oil. Stir in well.

When hot, spoon everything out into a large serving bowl. Throw on the Parmesan shavings, capers and the sprigs of Basil for decoration. Drizzle with Extra Virgin Olive oil. Salt and freshly ground pepper to taste.

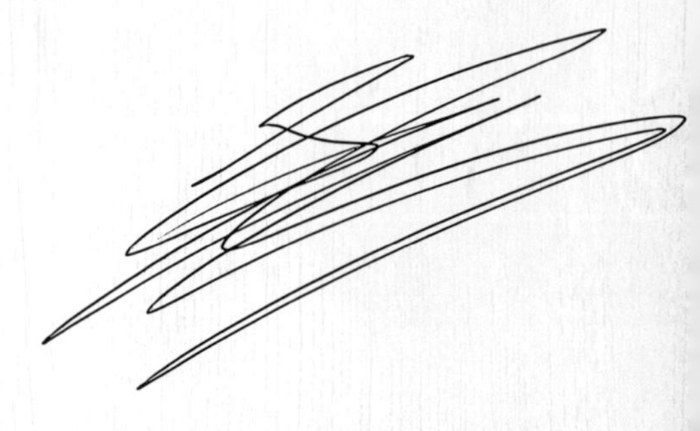

Chequers Steak Pie

by Rt. Hon. Gordon Brown MP

INGREDIENTS

Serves: approx. 8

300g diced chuck steak
1 large onion, diced
1 stick of celery
1 carrot
1 leek
100g oil
100g flour
1 litre beef stock
Worcestershire sauce
1 bay leaf
Salt and pepper
200g puff pastry
1 beaten egg

METHOD

Lightly brown the beef in oil and then remove the beef from the pan.

Add onion to the pan and fry.

Add flour and make a roux.

Heat the beef stock and then add slowly to the roux, ensuring that you stir continually.

Return beef to the pan and add a bay leaf, salt and pepper and seasonings to taste.

Add whole leek, carrot and celery, cover with a lid and cook slowly in the oven on a moderate heat until the meat is tender.

Remove leek, carrot and celery, add more seasoning if required, place in a suitable pie dish and allow to cool.

Roll out pastry to fit dish and place on top.

Brush pastry with beaten egg and rest for 10minutes before returning to a hot oven to cook until golden.

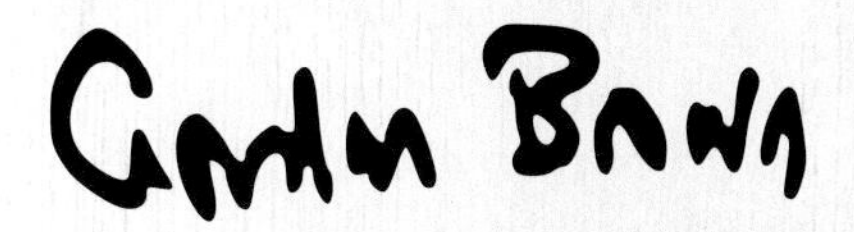

Rt. Hon. Gordon Brown MP is the Prime Minister

Spaghetti Bolognese

by James Cosmo

INGREDIENTS

1lb each minced beef and pork

4oz each streaky bacon and chicken livers

2 onions, chopped

4 garlic cloves, minced

2 tins chopped tomatoes

2 tins concentrated tomato purée

½ bottle red wine

Salt and pepper

½ teaspoon ground nutmeg

METHOD

Fry onions and garlic until soft.

Brown all the meats.

Add tomatoes, purée, wine and nutmeg.

Cook for 4 hours.

James Cosmo is an Actor

Best Ever Scones

by Deirdre Davis

INGREDIENTS

8oz self raising flour

2oz butter, straight from fridge

1 tsp salt

2oz caster sugar

5fl oz full fat milk

METHOD

Heat oven to 220°C.

Rub together flour and butter until it looks like breadcrumbs. Don't worry if it's not perfectly fine tho'.

Stir in sugar and salt. (You could add some dried fruit now too).

Pour in milk and mix with a knife until your mixture is a lump of not too gooey dough.

Turn out onto a floured surface and knead for a few minutes then flatten to about 2cm thickness.

Dip pastry cutter (or wine glass) in flour then use to cut out scones. Lay them on non-stick baking sheet.

Brush with milk and sprinkle with a little caster sugar.

Bake for 7-10 minutes until lovely and golden.

Serve warm if possible so that when you spread them with butter and jam, they melt on the way to your mouth!

Deirdre Davis

Deirdre Davis is an Actress in the popular soap River City

Shieldinch Smoked Haddock Soup

by Julie Duncanson

INGREDIENTS

Serves: 4

4 slices of smoked haddock

large carrot, finely diced

2 large potatoes, diced into 1cm cubes

¼ pint of single cream (or more if you wish)

2 oz butter

1 large onion, finely chopped

2 tbsp plain flour

small packet of fresh or defrosted prawns

fresh chopped parsley

(You can also add a tin of sweetcorn and/or some peas if you fancy!)

Julie Duncanson is an Actress in the popular soap River City

METHOD

Cook the fish in about a litre of water for around 8 mins or until opaque.

Lift the fish carefully from the pan and remove any skin or bones. Flake the fish into large chunks. Reserve the liquid stock.

Melt the butter in a large soup pan. Add chopped onion and fry gently until soft.

Add the flour then gradually add the stock. Add the carrot and potato and bring to the boil. Simmer until the vegetables are just soft. Add the flaked fish and the cream and heat but do not boil. Add the prawns and heat for another minute or so but do not cook too long or they will shrink and toughen.

Serve, sprinkled with parsley and with lots of crusty bread and butter.

My family love this recipe. It can be a meal on its own as it is very satisfying. If you are serving it as a first course then serve less and ease up on the bread and butter. Lovely as an alternative to steak pie for before the bells at New Year.

This is served daily in 'The Tall Ship' of course and it is Shona's special recipe.

Raymondo loves it!!!

Julie Duncanson
X

Scotch Broth

by Alex Ferguson

INGREDIENTS

Ham or Beef joint

Barley or Lentils

Carrots

Leeks

Onions

Various vegetables of your choice

METHOD

Take a ham or beef joint (personally, I prefer ham stock) and place in a pot of water, ¾ full.

Bring to the boil and then let it simmer until the meat is cooked. Let it cool down and once the fat has set on the top, take it off until you are left with a clear stock.

Then add your favourite vegetables which should include barley or lentils, carrots, leeks and onions. You can also add any vegetables of your choice such as cauliflower, broccoli, celery etc.

Basically this is a tasty broth which contains a mixture of everything. I was brought up on this and it has all the nourishment you need.

I hope that you enjoy this dish as much as I do!

Best wishes
Alex Ferguson

Sir Alex Ferguson CBE is the Manager of Manchester United FC

Banana Muffins

by Kirsty Gallacher

INGREDIENTS

250g self raising wholemeal flour

1 level teaspoon Baking Powder

3 fluid oz sunflower oil
or 50g melted butter

75g soft brown sugar

1 egg

2 medium ripe bananas

Walnut halves (optional)

METHOD

Place all the ingredients into a food processor except the walnuts and pulse until ingredients are mixed. Do not over mix.

Half fill muffin cases and place walnut on top. Bake at 160 -180°C (depending on oven type) for approx. 15 minutes.

Allow to cool on baking tray for 5 minutes and enjoy while warm.

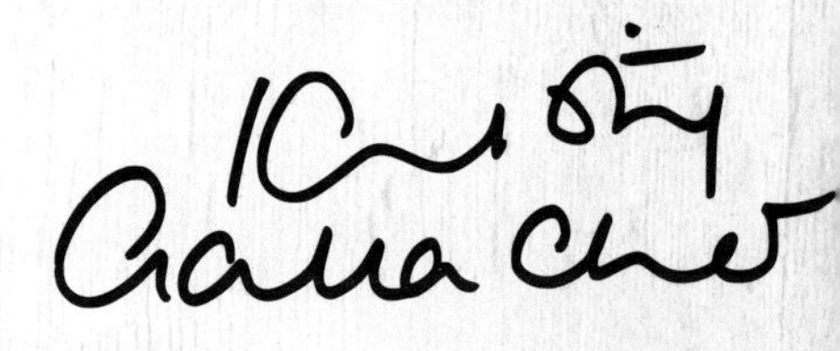

Kirsty Gallacher is a Television Presenter

Raspberry Cupcakes with Sparkly Buttercream Icing

by Lisa Gardner

INGREDIENTS

200g self-raising flour
2 tsp baking powder
200g unsalted butter
4 eggs
200g caster sugar
3 tbsp milk
50g ground almonds
150g punnet raspberries

Buttercream Icing

150g unsalted butter
200g icing sugar, sifted
1 tsp vanilla essence - optional

Lisa Gardner is an Actress in the popular soap River City

METHOD

Heat oven to 180°C - fan 160°C - gas 4.

Line a 12-hole muffin tin with cupcake cases. Tip the first 7 ingredients into a large bowl and beat with electric whisk until smooth. Fold the crushed raspberries through the batter. Defrosted raspberries work too but be sure to drain off the excess watery juice that comes off them.

Divide the batter between the cases (they should be about half full) and bake for 20-25 mins, until golden and just firm.

Remove the cupcakes from the oven and allow to cool a little before adding icing.

For the Icing

Break the butter up into small pieces into a mixing bowl. It helps if butter is at room temperature or you'll be mixing for hours! Beat it until it is smooth and creamy. Gradually add the icing sugar while mixing slowly until it is well combined. Taste as you go and if not sweet enough just add more icing sugar but using unsalted butter should help this. Add the vanilla essence and mix the icing vigorously until it is smooth and creamy.

Spread icing generously on cupcakes and sprinkle some edible glitter on top and et voilà! Eat quickly because they are nice warm. They should keep for two days max in tupperware and in fridge.

Roast Chicken with Sage and Onion Stuffing

by Iain Glen

INGREDIENTS

1 whole chicken

Salt and pepper

40g butter

Stuffing

4 chopped onions

10 sage leaves, chopped (reserve one leaf for garnish if desired)

125g breadcrumbs

1 beaten egg

50g butter

Iain Glen is an Actor

METHOD

Preheat oven 190°C.

Melt the butter and fry onions until softened.

Allow to cool and add the sage, breadcrumbs and season.

Add just enough egg to moisten the mixture.

Stuff the neck of the chicken then close the skin over the stuffing and secure with cocktail stick. (Any excess stuffing can be rolled into balls and cooked alongside the chicken for the last 25mins of cooking)

Place the chicken in a metal roasting pot, coat with butter and season to taste.

Cover loosely with foil.

Roast in centre of oven (30mins per 500g) and baste twice during cooking.

Around 20mins before end of cooking, remove foil and baste and turn up heat to 220°C to make the skin crispy.

Once cooked, allow to rest before carving. Ensure the juices run clear when pierced with a knife. If not, cook longer.

Garnish with a sprig of sage if desired.

Serve with Roast Potatoes, Bread Sauce, Gravy, Peas, Green beans and Carrots.

Iain Glen

Olé

by Andy Gray

INGREDIENTS

1lb mince

1 large onion, chopped

1 small tin sweetcorn

1 tin condensed cream of tomato soup

1 small can tomato purée

1 teaspoon chilli powder

Seasoning

8 ozs noodles, cooked and drained

4 ozs cheddar cheese, grated

METHOD

Fry the mince and onion in a heavy base pan.

Add all the ingredients to pan with exception of the noodles and cheese and mix well.

In an ovenproof dish, alternate layers of meat mixture and noodles.

Sprinkle the cheese on top.

Cook in oven 160°C for 35 minutes.

Andy Gray is a Football Presenter on Sky TV

Wine and Crème Fraîche Chicken

by Muriel Gray

INGREDIENTS

2x chicken breasts

White wine

Crème Fraîche

Chicken Stock

Coriander

Salt

Pepper

METHOD

Fry two chicken breasts in a pan with olive oil and butter.

Keep adding white wine and reducing. Add small amounts of chicken stock and reduce.

When chicken is browned both sides, remove and place in tin foil.

Add two large tablespoons of crème fraîche to the pan and a handful of freshly chopped coriander, salt and pepper.

Stir through until creamy then return chicken to sauce and serve with rice or creamed potatoes.

Only takes about fifteen minutes. Yum!

Muriel Gray

Muriel Gray is a Journalist and Television Presenter

Steak Pie

by John Greig

INGREDIENTS

2½ lbs round steak cut into 1 inch cubes

2 medium onions, roughly chopped

2 tablespoons plain flour to coat steak cubes

2 tablespoons oil

1 pint beef stock

Salt and pepper

Gravy granules or powder

1lb ready made puff pastry

John Greig MBE was Rangers FC's 1972 European Cup Winners' Cup winning Captain

METHOD

Toss steak cubes in flour until well coated.

Melt oil in saucepan and fry onions for a few minutes.

Add steak cubes and cook until meat is nicely browned.

Add remaining flour and stir well.

Season with salt and pepper.

Gradually stir in stock as well as granules or powder to give deeper colour to gravy.

Simmer gently for 2 hours or until meat is tender.

Pour into 3 pint pie dish.

Preheat oven to 180°C/Gas mark 6.

To prepare the pastry

Roll out puff pastry to fit pie dish, making sure that working surface is lightly floured.

Dampen the pie dish rim with cold water and place pastry on top, sealing well by pressing thumb firmly all round edge of dish.

Make steam hole in centre of pastry and score with blunt knife to make checked design on top.

Brush pastry with milk and chill in fridge.

Bake in oven for 45 minutes until browned and risen.

Serve with boiled potatoes and seasonal vegetables.

Pavlovas

by Sarah Heaney

INGREDIENTS

3 large egg whites

5 oz caster sugar

option of hazelnuts if you want (3 ground tablespoons)

Topping

10floz whipped cream

12 oz fruits i.e. strawberries, raspberries, blackberries and to top that you can also pop on some kiwi fruit for a splash of colour

Sarah Heaney is a Television Presenter

METHOD

Preheat oven to gas mark 2, 300°F or 150°C

First, lightly oil a baking tray then pop on a baking sheet.

In a bowl, whisk up the egg whites until quite firm i.e. you turn the bowl upside down without the mixture running out . (Do not overbeat the eggs)

When they are ready whisk in the sugar.

Take a metal tablespoon and spoon the meringue onto the baking sheet forming a 8 inch circle. Then spoon blobs next to each other so they join up and make a circle all around the edge.

Now using a knitting needle or a skewer make little swirls in the meringue sharply to leave tiny peaks.

Put into oven and turn down the heat to gas mark 1, 275°F/140°C and cook for 1hr then turn the heat off and leave the Pavlova inside until completely cold.

To serve, lift off meringue and peel away baking paper. Spread whipped cream on top then pop on fruit and, just before serving, dust with icing sugar.

Hmmm and loaded with calories yipee!

Sarah Heaney

Baked Pork Chops

by Stephen Hendry

INGREDIENTS

4 washed and dried pork chops

Juice of ½ an orange and ½ a lemon

1 teaspoon orange and lemon rind, grated

1/8 cup chopped parsley

1 tablespoon sugar

1 teaspoon mixed herbs

Pinch salt, pepper, nutmeg and paprika

Stephen Hendry MBE is a seven times World Champion Professional Snooker Player

METHOD

Put chops in a casserole dish.

Combine the rest of the ingredients to make the sauce.

Pour sauce over chops and cook in covered casserole dish for 1½ hours, removing lid for last 15 minutes.

Check a couple of times during cooking to ensure chops are well coated in the sauce.

Serve with new potatoes and your choice of vegetables.

Healthy Tropical Cashew Nut Rice Salad with Mango

by Lorraine Kelly

INGREDIENTS

350 calories, 10g fat

4 heaped tablespoons of cooked brown rice

1 tablespoon (15g) of salted cashew nuts

1 fresh mango, peeled

Juice of a lemon

1 tablespoon of chopped parsley

1 tablespoon of chopped chives

½ red pepper

small bunch of spring onions, finely sliced

lettuce leaves to serve with the salad

salt and pepper

Lorraine Kelly is a Television Presenter

METHOD

This salad is made in minutes and is so easy to whip up. You can buy ready cooked brown rice in tins or cook a batch yourself. Don't nibble on any extra cashews!

Heat a small frying pan on a moderate heat and roughly chop the cashew nuts on a board. Place the nuts in the heated frying pan to heat up slightly. This releases more flavour from the nuts so cuts down on the amount you have to use.

Meanwhile, cut the mango flesh into small cubes along with the red pepper. Mix the two ingredients in a bowl with the cooked brown rice. Now add the chopped chives, spring onions, parsley and lemon juice and continue to mix. Once the cashew nuts have toasted slightly, mix half of them into the salad and reserve the remainder for garnishing the top. Season to taste and serve in a suitable serving bowl with some lettuce garnish and finally sprinkle with the reserved cashew nuts.

Love Lorraine

Nellie Ogg's Kedgeree

by Claire Knight

INGREDIENTS

Serves: 4

1½ lb thick smoked haddock fillets or 700g smoked mackerel

4oz butter

1 carrot, 1 red pepper and 1 onion, chopped

¾ level teaspoon hot (madras) curry powder

long grain white rice measured up to the 8 fl oz level in a measuring jug

3 hard boiled eggs, chopped

3 heaped tablespoons fresh chopped parsley

1 tablespoon lemon juice

salt and freshly milled black pepper

Claire Knight is an Actress in the popular soap River City

METHOD

Nellie Ogg was my Grandma. A great cook and a very funny and young gran. This was my favourite dish as a young child coming home from school.

Put the haddock/mackerel fillets in a pan and cover them with 1pint cold water.

Bring to the boil then put on a lid and simmer gently for about 8mins.

Drain off the water into a measuring jug and put to one side.

If the fish needs skinned, now is the time to gently peel off the skins and discard. (Keep the cooked fish warm by wrapping in tin foil until you have prepared the rest of the ingredients).

Now, using the same saucepan, melt 2oz of the butter and soften the onion, carrot and pepper in it for 5mins.

Next stir in the curry powder, cook for a wee minute then stir in the measured rice and add 16fl oz of the haddock cooking water. Stir once then, when it comes up to simmering point, cover with a tight-fitting lid and cook very gently for 15mins.

When the rice is ready, remove it from the heat. Flake the fish which you wrapped in tinfoil earlier and add to the rice along with the hard boiled eggs, parsley, lemon juice and the remaining 2oz butter.

Now turn off the heat and leave for 5mins.

Tip out in to 4 bowls. I like to add some lemon wedges and lots of freshly ground black pepper. Serve with hot buttered toast.

Claire Knight

Chocolate Voluptas

by Simone Lahbib

INGREDIENTS

Serves: 10-12

675g dark chocolate (70% cocoa)

450g unsalted butter

10 organic eggs

450g caster sugar

Crème fraîche and raspberries to serve

Simone Lahbib is an Actress

METHOD

Preheat oven to 160°C.

Line a 27cm spring form cake tin with foil.

Place the chocolate and butter in bowl over a saucepan of simmering water until melted.

Remove from heat and allow to cool.

Place eggs and sugar in a large bowl and beat until thickened.

Fold the cooled chocolate mixture into egg mixture, stirring until well combined.

Pour into the prepared cake tin then place in a large baking tray and pour boiling water into the tray ¾ of the way up the sides of the cake tin.

Bake in the oven for 1 hour until set.

Leave to cool completely before turning out.

Serve with a dollop of crème fraîche and raspberries/ strawberries.

...Enjoy! x

Simone Lahbib

Quick, Simple and Tasty Turkey Burger

by Lulu

INGREDIENTS

Serves: 4

1lb turkey mince

1 finely chopped onion

½ clove of garlic, very finely chopped

1 handful of fresh parsley

Salt and pepper

1 pinch of Cajun spice

METHOD

Place all ingredients in a bowl.

Mix everything together with your hands until the mix is even.

Separate into four balls and flatten down with your hands into a burger shape.

Place under a medium heat grill or into a frying pan and cook for 2½ minutes on each side until browned and cooked through.

Serve with salad and a bun, adding cheese, ketchup, mustard or any condiment you fancy…Delicious!

Lulu

Lulu is a Singer / Songwriter

Pete's Salad

by Amy Macdonald

INGREDIENTS

Cos lettuce
Tomatoes
Cucumber
Celery
Beetroot
Seedless grapes
Crisp Apples like Cox
Block of Feta cheese
Lemon juice

METHOD

While Amy was recording her debut album, she stayed in London with her Manager/Producer, Pete Wilkinson and his wife Sarah. During her stay, she was introduced to Pete's salad dish which she now calls Pete's Salad.

It is safe to say Pete is not a precision chef (!) so there is no delicate method to preparing this. Simply chop, slice or dice the ingredients to your preference.

Always use very fresh ingredients and wash everything thoroughly. This is a great healthy accompaniment to pizza!

Amy Macdonald is a Singer / Songwriter

Kipper Tart

by Rob Maclean

INGREDIENTS

Savoury pastry case

40g unsalted butter

Pinch ground cumin

Teaspoon turmeric

Pinch cayenne and ground cinnamon

Juice of lemon

200g kipper fillets, skinned, boned and flaked

120g mascarpone

Chopped fresh parsley

METHOD

Melt butter, add cumin, turmeric, cayenne and cinnamon and stir-fry for 1 minute.

Add lemon juice and kipper fillets and cook 5 minutes, stirring constantly.

Cool slightly.

Mix kippers with mascarpone and fill pastry case.

Sprinkle with parsley, heat gently for 20 minutes or serve at room temperature.

Rob Maclean is a Television Presenter

Grilled Brown Trout with New Potatoes and Salad

by Hans Matheson

This simple dish is one of my favourites inspired by fond memories of going fishing on Loch Breugach with my brother Will and our Grandpa Bill Maclean on the Isle of Lewis. These were truly magical days. There is nothing quite like coming home with fresh fish you have caught and Grandma Belle cooking them that same evening served with new potatoes, lettuce and parsley straight from the garden.

METHOD

Clean and prepare fish, removing the back bone and opening it out flat.

Dot with knobs of butter and season with salt and pepper.

Place under a moderate grill for about 5 to 8 minutes.

Serve with new potatoes, crisp green salad, fresh tomatoes, chopped parsley and a wedge of lemon.

Hope you enjoy it as much as I do!

Hans Matheson

Hans Matheson is an Actor.

Risotto

by Eileen McCallum

INGREDIENTS

1 medium onion, chopped

2oz butter

1¾pints chicken or vegetable stock

1 small glass dry white wine (optional)

10oz Arborio rice

2oz freshly grated parmesan cheese

black pepper

METHOD

In a large pan, fry the onion in half the butter until soft.

In a separate pan, heat the stock and keep simmering.

Add the wine to the fried onion, turn up heat and boil to reduce it.

Add the rice and stir well to coat the grains.

Then, using a ladle, add the stock gradually over a medium heat, stirring all the time as the liquid is absorbed. The rice should be creamy but still 'al dente'. Be prepared to stand and stir for about 20minutes.

Add the remaining butter, grated parmesan and black pepper and serve piping hot with a green salad.

This is a basic risotto. I almost always add mushrooms – a handful of dried porcini soaked in hot water for 20 minutes and some chopped fresh mushrooms fried and added at the end. (Add the water from the dried mushrooms with the stock.)

Any left over cooked chicken makes a more substantial meal.

Eileen McCallum

Eileen McCallum is an actress presently appearing in River City

Mince and Potatoes with Dough Balls

by Billy McNeill

INGREDIENTS

1lb of Aberdeen Angus Minced Beef

1 cup water

1 Oxo beef stock cube

Olive oil

1 onion, chopped

2 large carrots, chopped

Half a turnip, chopped

For Dough Balls

¼ lb self raising flour

½ teaspoon baking powder

Salt and pepper

2 ozs Atora suet

METHOD

Put oil in pan and fry onion until translucent then add mince and brown.

Mash down mince with back of fork and add the beef stock and water.

Add carrot and turnip, mix well and simmer until vegetables are softened.

Meanwhile, prepare the dough balls.

Sieve self raising flour and baking powder into bowl.

Add seasoning to taste and Atora suet.

Use cold water to mix to a fairly thin dough (not too runny).

Shape into balls and drop into mince (add more water if required so dough balls are well coated).

Simmer mince and dough balls for a further 30 minutes before serving.

Serving

Most people like mashed potatoes with their mince but I like it served with whole Golden Wonder potatoes and a dough ball.

Billy McNeill MBE was Celtic FC's 1967 European Cup winning Captain

Fish Pie

by Willie Miller

INGREDIENTS

100g mature cheddar cheese, grated
3 tablespoons wholegrain mustard
350g skinless cod fillet
225g skinless salmon fillet
250g pack mixed seafood cocktail
300ml fish stock
900g potatoes
2 bay leaves
25g butter
1 tablespoon cornflour
4 tablespoons single cream
15g fresh chives
Fresh ground black pepper

Willie Miller MBE was Aberdeen FC's 1983 European Cup Winners' Cup winning Captain

METHOD

Preheat oven to 220°C/425°F

Place the cod and salmon in a shallow pan with bay leaves and pour over stock.

Bring to the boil, cover and simmer for approx. 10 minutes until the fish is just cooked. Remove from heat and set to one side.

Meanwhile, cut the potatoes into small chunks, cook until tender and drain well.

Add the butter to the potatoes and mash until smooth.

Add the mustard, half the cheese and using scissors, snip in the chives. Add the seasoning, mix well and set to one side.

Drain the fish, reserving the stock and flake into bite size pieces. Mix with the seafood and place in deep ovenproof gratin dish. Discard the bay leaves from the stock.

Blend the cornflour with a little stock and place in a saucepan. Pour in the remaining stock and bring to the boil, stirring until thick and clear.

Remove from the heat and stir in the cream. Adjust seasoning.

Spoon the sauce over the fish, making sure it is all covered.

Spoon the potato over the top to cover the fish completely and sprinkle over remaining cheese.

Bake for 25-30 minutes until golden, bubbling and hot and serve immediately.

Monty's Beef Stir-fry

by Colin Montgomerie

INGREDIENTS

1 tbsp Chilli oil

1 tbsp Soy sauce

1 Crushed garlic clove

1 Large red Chilli, seeded and chopped

400g Lean fillet steak cut into strips

Broccoli

Mange touts

1 Red pepper, seeded and chopped

METHOD

Pour the chilli oil into a medium sized bowl. Add soy sauce and garlic.

Cut up the fillet of beef into strips and add to the marinade in the bowl.

Heat the oil in a wok until very hot.

Add the fillet strips for 3-4 mins then set aside.

Add the broccoli, mange touts, red chilli and red pepper along with 2 tbsp of water.

Stir fry for 6 mins then add the fillet strips.

Enjoy!

Colin Montgomerie OBE is a Professional Golfer

Hearty Lentil Broth

by Rt. Hon. Jim Murphy MP

INGREDIENTS

1 onion, chopped
1 large potato, peeled and chopped
6 carrots, peeled and chopped
500g red lentils, washed
2.5 pints vegetable stock
1 tablespoon tomato sauce
1 teaspoon brown sauce
salt and pepper

METHOD

Sautée onions in a little butter.

Add lentils.

Add potato, carrot and stock and stir.

Bring to the boil.

Simmer for 30 minutes until vegetables are tender.

Add both the brown and tomato sauce.

Add salt and pepper.

Garnish with 2 tablespoons of finely chopped flat leaf parsley.

Serve with crusty loaf.

Jim Murphy

Rt. Hon. Jim Murphy MP is the Secretary of State for Scotland

Hot Smoked Salmon Fishcake

by Nick Nairn

INGREDIENTS

600g hot smoked salmon
300g mash (King Edwards or Maris Pipers)
2 spring onions
juice of 1 lemon
Maldon salt
freshly ground black pepper
seasoned flour for coating
olive oil for frying
extra olive oil for drizzling

Tomato salsa

250g cherry tomatoes, cut into halves
1/2 small red onion, peeled and finely diced
1 garlic clove, peeled and finely diced
1 small red chilli, sliced diagonally and seeded
2 tbsp chopped fresh basil
1 tbsp Chardonnay or white wine vinegar
3 tbsp extra virgin olive oil
Maldon sea salt and freshly ground black pepper

Nick Nairn is a Celebrity Chef

METHOD

For the salsa, mix all the ingredients together, cover and set aside while you make the fishcakes.

Put the mash into a large mixing bowl and add the flaked salmon and spring onions. Squeeze the lemon juice into the mix. Fold together with a wooden spoon until the fish is well mixed through. Taste and adjust the seasoning if necessary.

Divide the mixture equally into eight and shape into cricket balls, then using the palm of your hand, gently flatten them to make cake shapes. Sift the flour onto a large bowl or plate. Roll the fishcakes in the flour until evenly coated. Lift and pat gently to remove excess flour.

Heat a medium frying pan to hot. Add the olive oil and heat, swirling it around a little to coat the bottom of the pan. Carefully slide 4 fishcakes into the pan. Turn the heat down to medium and cook for about 5 minutes until a nice brown crust has formed. As always if you're looking to get a nice crust, don't be tempted to fiddle with the cakes. Carefully turn the cakes over and fry for another five minutes. Lift out of the pan and drain on kitchen paper.

To serve, place a dollop of salsa in the centre of each plate, place a fishcake on top and drizzle round a little olive oil.

Nick Nairn

Trout On Lime and Coriander

by Barbara Rafferty

INGREDIENTS

Serves: 4

4 Scottish trout fillets

1tbsp olive oil

2 limes

bunch of coriander (2tbsp)

sea salt and pepper

METHOD

Preheat oven to 190°C (gas mark 5).

Place fillets on lightly oiled baking tray.

Squeeze juice of one lime over the fillets. Season lightly with salt and more generously with pepper. Scatter the lovely aromatic coriander on top. (Keep the lime shells and put in with trout and cover with tin foil).

Bake in the oven for approx. 8-10 mins. Check after 5 mins that it is not overcooked.

Garnish with the other limes. Serve with baby new potatoes and rocket salad – yummy – enjoy!

Barbara Rafferty is an Actress

Veggie Soup

by Ian Rankin

INGREDIENTS

Any vegetables you have to hand

Stock cube or liquid stock

Water

METHOD

Chop an onion and fry in a cooking pot in some vegetable oil.

Chop vegetables (leek, diced potato, carrots, cabbage, diced parsnips etc).

Add to pot and gently fry for five minutes.

Add a pint or two of boiling water and bring to boil then simmer for 20 minutes, having added 1 or 2 stock cubes or liquid stock.

Once cooked, soup can be liquidised.

You can then lie to your kids by telling them it only contains their favourite veg! In my son's case, leek and potato.

Ian Rankin OBE is an Author

Paella of Pork, Chorizo and Spinach

by Derek Riddell

INGREDIENTS

Serves: 4 - main, 6 - starter

7 tablespoons of olive oil

350g pork fillet, halved lengthways then sliced roughly into thin strips

120g mild chorizo

2 large Spanish onions, finely chopped

1 large green pepper, halved, seeded and finely chopped

4 garlic cloves, finely chopped

250g of paella or Arborio rice

1 teaspoon sweet smoked Spanish paprika

900mls hot chicken stock

500g spinach, washed and drained

Lemon wedges

Salt and pepper

Derek Riddell is an Actor

METHOD

In a frying pan heat olive oil over a high heat then stir fry the pork for a few seconds so it's still a little undercooked.

Season with salt and pepper, remove from the pan and put to one side.

Turn down heat to a low to medium temperature and fry the chorizo for a minute.

Add the onion, green pepper and cook for 20 minutes, stirring occasionally.

Add the garlic and cook for a further 5-10 minutes. At this point the mixture should have caramelised and taste sweet.

Stir the rice into the pan and coat it all in the mixture for a minute

(N.B. All these stages can be done in advance. The next stage requires about 20 minutes further cooking time).

Season with salt and a little pepper.

Add paprika, hot stock and simmer for 15 minutes or until there is just a thin layer of liquid around the rice.

Meanwhile, in a large saucepan or wok, briefly wilt the spinach with a little salt either by braising or steaming and put to one side with the pork fillet.

Finally scatter the pork then spinach over the rice. With the back of a spoon push the pork and spinach partially into the oily liquid that remains at the bottom of the pan.

Cover with foil, let it sit for 3-5 minutes and serve with lemon wedges and tomato salad.

Porridge à la Cinnamon/Slimmers

by Tony Roper

INGREDIENTS

½ cup of porridge oats

1 dessertspoon cinnamon

1 teaspoon grated ginger

1 banana

1 tablespoon soya cream eg. Alpro

1 tablespoon grape nuts (optional)

skimmed milk

METHOD

Pour half a cup of porridge oats into a bowl and mix in grape nuts and cinnamon powder.

Cover with skimmed milk.

Add sliced banana and partly cover the top of dish.

Place in microwave for approx. 3 minutes or until porridge has risen to rim of bowl then add soya cream.

Delicious, filling, healthy and around 200 calories!

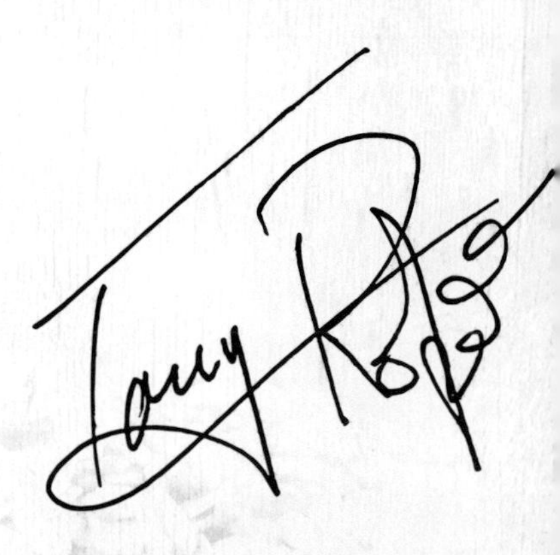

Tony Roper is an Actor, Author, Playwright and Director

Cullen Skink

by The Rt. Hon. Alex Salmond MSP

INGREDIENTS

2 medium smoked haddock or Finnan haddock or one large haddock on the bone.

2 medium onions

Pint of milk

1lb potatoes

2oz butter

METHOD

Put fish in cold water, enough to cover.

Bring to the boil and simmer for 10 minutes.

Take out fish and remove bones and skin and then flake fish.

Cook onions in the butter, taking care not to brown the onion.

Cook potatoes and mash with a knob of butter.

Add liquid from fish, pint of milk and onion.

Salt, pepper and small amount of parsley may be added to taste.

Alex Salmond

Rt. Hon. Alex Salmond MSP is the First Minister of Scotland

Kedgeree

by Carol Smillie

INGREDIENTS

Fish stock cubes
3 pieces smoked haddock
curry powder
plain rice
coriander
1 onion
butter

METHOD

Chop up the onion and fry in a large pan in butter until it becomes soft and translucent.

Add a teaspoon of curry powder.

Add the haddock pieces and cover with fish stock.

Allow to simmer for 10mins or so until fish is cooked.

Break up the fish loosely with a fork and add the rice (top up the stock if necessary to keep the dish juicy).

Chop up the coriander roughly and add.

Soft boil 4 eggs for 7mins, take the shells off and quarter them.

Sprinkle on top of each portion (do not mix through as they will break up too much).

Sprinkle with black pepper and serve.

Carol Smillie

Carol Smillie is a Television Presenter

Penne Arrabbiata

by Walter Smith

INGREDIENTS

Serves: 4-6

Control the heat of the dish by using more or less hot red pepper.

¼ cup extra virgin olive oil

3 large garlic cloves, minced

1½lbs tomatoes, preferably plum tomatoes, peeled and seeded and coarsely chopped

2 x 14.5oz (1 x 28oz) can imported Italian tomatoes with their juice, chopped

1 or 2 dried hot red chillies, broken into pieces or hot red pepper flakes

salt to taste

1 lb penne or other short thick round pasta

5 quarts water

Walter Smith OBE is Manager of Rangers FC

METHOD

Heat the oil in a heavy saucepan over medium-high heat and sauté the garlic, stirring constantly until it is just beginning to turn golden – about 10 minutes.

Add the tomatoes and chillies, reduce the heat to medium-low and continue cooking until the tomatoes are soft and the sauce is dense but not pureed – about 20 minutes.

Remove from the heat and taste for seasoning, adding more salt if necessary.

Cook the pasta.

Drain thoroughly, turn into a warm serving bowl and pour the sauce over it.

Serve immediately.

Baked Lemon and Polenta Cake

by Sharleen Spiteri

INGREDIENTS

225g unsalted butter
225g caster sugar
225g ground almonds
1 vanilla pod
3 eggs
2 lemons (juice and zest)
225g polenta
10g baking powder
pinch salt

METHOD

Cream together the butter and sugar.

Add in the ground almonds and vanilla seeds.

Slowly beat in the eggs one by one.

Pour in the lemon juice and zest.

Fold in the polenta, a pinch of salt and the baking powder.

Pour mixture into a buttered cake tin and bake at 160°C for 45-55 minutes.

Sharleen Spiteri is a Singer / Songwriter

Pasta with Pancetta and Courgette

by Kirsty Wark

INGREDIENTS

Pasta (preferably dried)
1 red onion
garlic
Pancetta
1 courgette
1 tbsp Crème fraîche
1 tsp Dijon mustard
Black pepper

METHOD

Here is a recipe for a quick and delicious pasta.

Sauté one chopped red onion in a pan with some chopped garlic and pancetta pieces and then set aside.

Prepare pasta (preferably dried) and while doing that, plunge a shredded courgette into a pan of boiling water for a minute, drain and add to onion and pancetta mix.

Drain pasta when al dente and then add to it one tablespoon of crème fraîche mixed with a teaspoon Dijon mustard and a generous amount of black pepper.

Then add the sautéed mix to it.

Kirsty Wark

Kirsty Wark is a Journalist and Television Presenter

Bolognese Meat Sauce

by Jonathan Watson

INGREDIENTS

Serves: 4-6

40g butter

2 tablespoons olive oil

1 onion, chopped

1 celery stick, chopped

1 carrot, chopped

250g/9oz minced steak

1 tablespoon concentrated tomato puree

salt and pepper

METHOD

This is the best Bolognese sauce...ever!

Heat the butter and olive oil in a small saucepan, and add the onion, celery, carrot and ground steak. Season with salt and pepper to taste.

Mix well and cook over a low heat for a few minutes, until the vegetables have softened and the meat starts to brown.

Mix the tomato puree with a little water to dilute and add to the saucepan.

Cover and cook over a very low heat for an hour and a half, adding a little water if the sauce seems to be drying out.

Serve with tagliatelle and grated Pecorino cheese...and a large glass of Italian Red!

Jonathan Watson

Jonathan Watson is a Television Comedy Actor

Meringues

by Bob Wilson

INGREDIENTS

4 egg whites (large)

4 oz granulated sugar

4 oz caster sugar

METHOD

Whip egg whites until holding shape but not too dry. Gradually add granulated sugar and continue to whip. When able to turn bowl upside down without mixture falling out, gently fold in rest of caster sugar.

With two dessert spoons, shape mixture into oval balls and lay on baking tray lined with non-stick parchment.

Put in oven at 150°C for 1 hour then turn down to 100°C and leave for another 4 hours. Turn off heat and allow meringues to cool in oven. Store in airtight tin.

Meringues may be sandwiched together with whipped double cream. Alternatively, coat flat bottom of each meringue with melted chocolate and allow to set then sandwich together with whipped cream.

Photograph courtesy of Chris George, 24SE7EN Magazine

Bob Wilson OBE is a former Scotland Goalkeeper and Television Presenter

Restaurants

Moules Marinière

by Paul Burns, *Head Chef*, The Airds Hotel & Restaurant

INGREDIENTS

1kg Fresh Mussels - clean
1 Small Onion, finely chopped
1Clove of Garlic, sliced
White of 1 Leek, finely sliced
1 Medium Carrot, cut into thin strips
200ml White Wine
200ml Vegetable Stock
up to 200ml Double Cream
Chopped Parsley & ground Black Pepper to finish

METHOD

In a large pan start to reduce the wine by 2/3rds and add the vegetable stock and reduce a little.

Add the garlic and the rest of the vegetables.

Simmer gently for 30 seconds.

Add a little cream and all the mussels.

Place lid on pan to allow the steam to open the mussels (approx. 5-7 mins).

Place in bowls with some of the stock.

Sprinkle with parsley and grind black pepper on top.

Never force open Mussels that refuse to open during cooking

Chocolate Mielie Meal Pudding

By Pete Gottgens, *Head Chef / Owner*, Ardeonaig Hotel & Restaurant

INGREDIENTS

20 Eggs

20 Egg yolks

500g Caster Sugar

1kg Dark cooking Chocolate, chopped

1kg unsalted Butter, cut into cubes

30g Mielie Meal (Grind the Mielie Meal in a pestle mortar)

Pinch Salt

120g Plain flour

METHOD

The mixture fills approximately 25-30 dariol moulds.

Melt the chocolate and butter over a double boiler on a low heat, stirring occasionally with a spatula.

Mix the eggs, egg yolks and caster sugar, until the sugar is about dissolved.

While the chocolate is melting, you can spray the dariol moulds with wax spray and then turn them over onto a cloth to catch the excess grease.

When the chocolate mix is melted, mix slowly into the egg mixture.

Mix the ground mielie meal, flour and salt.

Whisk the mielie meal, flour and salt into the chocolate mixture gradually (you don't have to use all the flour mix).

Fill the moulds ¾ full with the chocolate mixture and bake at 200°C until just firm on top (approx. 7 minutes).

The centre of the pudding will be liquid.

Ardeonaig Hotel & Restaurant, South Road Loch Tay, Ardeonaig, FK21 8SU
Tel 01567 820400
Email info@ardeonaighotel.co.uk www.ardeonaighotel.co.uk

Oxtail Risotto with Roasted Salsify and Crisp Parsley

By Gary Goldie, *Head Chef*, Ardanaiseig Hotel

INGREDIENTS

Serves:
8 starters or 4 main courses

250g x Arborio Risotto rice

3x Shallots(finely chopped)

1x litre Veal stock

400ml of Chicken stock

150ml of Red Wine

2x tbsp finely grated fresh Parmesan Cheese

2x Salsify

Flour/butter

1x tbsp Flat leaf Parsley and sprigs for garnish

For the marinade

1x Oxtail, about 1.3kg

1x Bottle of red wine, saving 150ml for risotto
(use a wine acceptable for drinking like Cabernet Sauvignon)

1x Onion

2x Carrots

1x Leek (all veg roughly chopped)

3x Cloves of bashed Garlic

2x Sprigs of Thyme

1x Bay Leaf

METHOD

Oxtails

Slice the Oxtail in-between the bones, the knife slices easily through, and then marinade the slices overnight in the wine, vegetables and herbs.

Drain the oxtail and vegetables in a colander saving the wine, separate the oxtail from the vegetables and season it with salt and pepper. Heat a large pan to very hot on your hob, add oil and fry off the oxtail, caramelising it a little and remove to a tray. Do it in stages if need be. Next roast the vegetables in the same still hot pan to caramelise, then deglaze the pan with the wine and reduce it by half, skimming frequently. Now add the stock and bring to the boil and finally add the oxtail, patting it dry of fat with a cloth and make sure the stock covers it.

Tinfoil the pan or if your oven is not big enough, transfer it to a large deep oven dish, tinfoil that and braise in the oven at 160°C for 4 hours until the meat falls off the bone. Remove the oxtail from the pot to a tray, skim well and pass off the stock. When the oxtail cools to touch, carefully remove the meat from the bone, not breaking it up too much, and discard the bones.

Reduce a third the stock, skimming off the fat, until it becomes thick, and put in the picked meat, you might not need it all, you should have like an oxtail stew, make this part to be ready whilst your rice is cooking.

Crisp Parsley

Tightly cling film a sturdy plate to go in the microwave, so the cling film is flat over the plate.

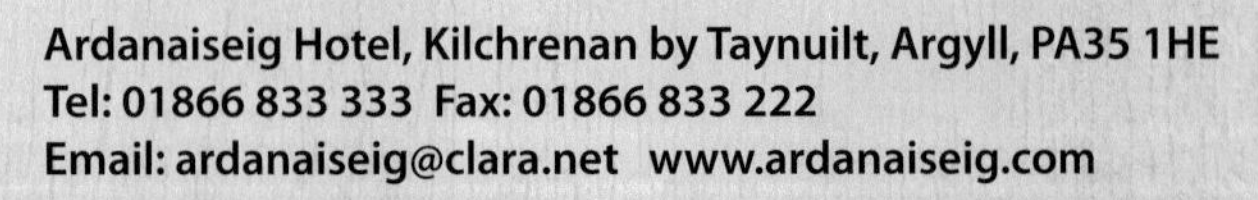
Ardanaiseig Hotel, Kilchrenan by Taynuilt, Argyll, PA35 1HE
Tel: 01866 833 333 Fax: 01866 833 222
Email: ardanaiseig@clara.net www.ardanaiseig.com

Dip nice sprigs, one by one, of your parsley in vegetable oil and, letting it drip off, place on your plate and lay out flat.

Microwave the plate for 1 minute, let it sit to cool a bit and see if its crispy by picking it up by the stalk. If it flops, give it another 30 seconds and repeat until it's ready, when it holds its shape. Leave it to cool and just before serving, season it with the tiniest bit of salt.

Salsify

Boil 1.5 litres of water in pot, add salt and whisk in a handful of flour to make a blanc.

Squeeze a lemon onto a tray.

Peel salsify and roll in lemon juice.

Cut in half to fit in pot and cook, adding the lemon juice and cook for about 20 minutes until its tender.

Cut diagonally into 3-4 cm sticks and pan-roast in butter to golden brown, season with salt and pepper and set aside on a silver tray. This is ready now but can be re-warmed under the grill or in a hot oven.

To make the risotto

Fry the shallot in olive oil in a heavy based pan until translucent, then add risotto rice and fry for a minute more. Next add 150ml of red wine and reduce it so just the rice remains.

Now add half the chicken stock and simmer for a few minutes, reducing and stirring occasionally. Add more stock a bit at a time, making sure the rice is still a bit firm and the stock is just binding it together.

Now add some oxtail stock, some at a time, still stirring and loosely boiling. Add salt and heavily season with pepper, taste, making sure your rice is nice and still a little firm. If it's too hard keep adding oxtail stock and stirring.

To finish

Fold your stewed oxtail meat into the rice, gently, leaving the meat in big chunks, then combine in the parsley and parmesan, adjust the seasoning and transfer to your serving bowls, with cutters to shape if you want and top with the salsify and crisp parsley.

CHEFS NOTE

Use a beef stock or good bouillon if you can't get veal or miss out the parmesan if you wish. It's really up to you to judge this recipe to how you like it. Serve it as a starter or a main course, maybe with salad on the side. Any leftover meat or stock can be kept and used later.

Wild Venison Saddle, Rosti Potato, Chestnuts & Wild Mushrooms

By Neil Forbes, *Head Chef*, Atrium

INGREDIENTS

Serves: 4

4 x 180 Gram Pieces of Wild Roe Deer or Red Venison (ask your game dealer to do this for you)

4 Medium Potatoes, Peeled & Grated

1 Handful of Peeled Chestnuts

200 Grams Mixed Wild Mushrooms, Cleaned & Chopped

1 Handful of Spinach, Washed & Picked

1 Handful of Wild Garlic, Washed & Picked

Olive Oil

Salt & Pepper

Unsalted Butter

1 Litre Good Game Stock

1 Litre Good Beef Stock

½ Bottle Red Wine

1 Shallot

1 Tablespoon Red Currant Jelly

METHOD

In a large pot reduce the red wine, chopped shallot and red currant jelly until it resembles jam. Add the stocks and reduce until it is of a sauce consistency

In a hot pan fry the Venison pieces in a little oil with salt and pepper, set to one side

To make the Rostis

Using 4 small blini pans* fry the grated potatoes with salt and pepper until golden brown on both sides using a little oil and butter. Place in oven to crisp. (*Alternatively use a frying pan, making 4 'discs' of grated potato)

In a frying pan sauté the mushrooms and chestnuts in a little butter

Place Venison in a very hot oven for 5-10 minutes until it gives a little when you touch the meat. Allow to rest

Meanwhile, wilt the spinach and wild garlic together in a pot with salt, pepper and butter

On 4 warm plates place the spinach and wild garlic in the centre, place a rosti on top, arrange the mushrooms and chestnuts around the outside

Slice the Venison and place onto the rosti, then drizzle sauce around and a little over the Venison. Serve immediately

ATRIUM

Atrium, 10 Cambridge St, Edinburgh, EH1 2ED
Tel: +44 (0)131 228 8882 Fax: +44 (0)131 228 8808
Email: eat@atriumrestaurant.co.uk www.atriumrestaurant.co.uk

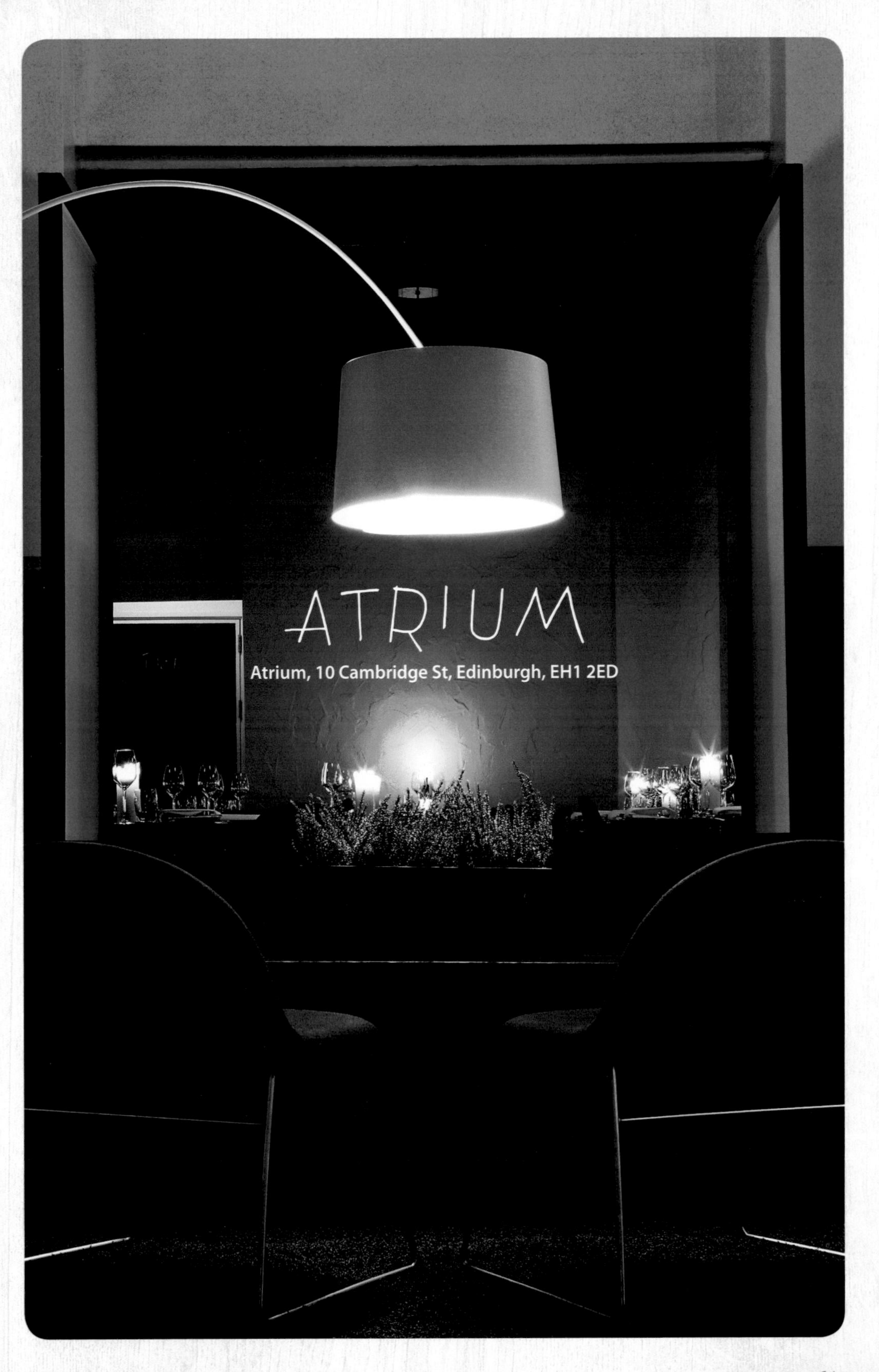
ATRIUM
Atrium, 10 Cambridge St, Edinburgh, EH1 2ED

Cannon of Lamb with a Ragout of Kidneys and Ratatouille

by Ian McAndrew, *Chef Proprietor*, Blackaddie Country House Hotel

INGREDIENTS

Serves: 4

2 cannons of lamb from the best end, each to weigh 170-180g fully trimmed

2 lambs kidneys

10g chopped shallot

20ml oil

20g unsalted butter

30ml port

30ml red wine

225ml lamb/veal jus

200g picked leaf spinach

Ratatouille

1 small courgette, outside cut into a 1cm dice, discard centre

¼ small aubergine, outside cut into a 1cm dice, discard centre

½ small red onion, cut into a 1cm dice

½ red pepper, deseeded and cut into a 1cm dice

½ yellow pepper, deseeded and cut into a 1cm dice

1 clove garlic, crushed

20ml olive oil

25g tomato puree

4 portions of gratin Dauphinoise to serve with the dish (optional)

METHOD

Cut the kidneys in half and remove their core. Very thinly slice.

Heat a frying pan and when hot add 5g of the butter. Lightly sweat the chopped shallots without colouring and until they start to soften, then add the port and red wine. Reduce this over a high heat until almost gone. Meanwhile, heat 10ml of the oil in a frying pan. Once it starts to smoke, add 5g of the butter, add the slices of kidney and fry very quickly on full heat until sealed and lightly browned. Drain immediately.

Once the wine and port has reduced,add the lamb/veal jus and continue to reduce until syrupy. Add the well-drained kidneys and keep warm.

To make the ratatouille, heat the 20ml of olive oil. When very hot but not quite smoking, add the onions and garlic. Cook these very quickly for about one minute then add the peppers and cook for a further minute very fast, stirring frequently to prevent burning. Then add the aubergines and cook for a further minute before adding the courgettes. Cook for one more minute then stir in the tomato puree. Cook for a final minute then remove from the heat.

Heat a further 10ml of oil in a frying pan and when hot add 5g of butter. Lightly season the cannons of lamb then fry them in the hot fat for about 6 minutes, browning well on all sides until cooked but still pink. Remove from the pan and keep in a warm place to rest for 5 minutes.

Heat the remaining 5g of butter and quickly cook the spinach. Once hot, season and drain well.

Fill a cutter with ratatouille and place off to one side of each plate. Arrange the spinach on the plate. Spoon the kidney ragout onto the plates. Carve each cannon into six thick slices and place three pieces of lamb on each plate on the kidneys.

Blackaddie House Hotel, Sanquhar, Dumfriesshire, DG4 6JJ
Tel: 01659 50270 Fax: 01659 50900
Email: info@blackaddiehotel.co.uk www.blackaddiehotel.co.uk

Peterhead Fishcake, Lanark Valley Tomatoes & Lemon Mayo

By Adrian Knibbs, *Head Chef* & Neil Forbes, *Head Chef*, Blue

INGREDIENTS

Serves: 4

250 Gram Diced Mixed Fish (Salmon, Monkfish, Coley, Langoustine)

1 Large Potato (Mashed)

Handful of Spring Onions, Finely Chopped

Zest & Juice of 1 Lemon & 1 Lime

1 Tablespoon Capers, Chopped

1 Tablespoon Chives, Chopped

1 Teaspoon Flat Parsley, Chopped

1 Large Handful of Local Yellow & Red Cherry Tomatoes

1 Red Onion, Finely Chopped

Olive Oil

Salt & Pepper

100 Gram Fresh Breadcrumbs

1 Egg

Handful Flour

Splash of Milk

Baby Salad Leaves for Garnish

METHOD

Cook your fish in a moderate oven until just cooked and add to a bowl.

Add your mashed potato, half the spring onions, capers, herbs, half of the zest, salt and pepper.

Give this a good mix and season if needed.

Refrigerate for 1 hour.

Meanwhile, cut the tomatoes in half and put in a bowl with the remaining spring onions, a splash of olive oil, salt and pepper. Put to one side.

Remove the fishcake mix from the fridge and mould into little cake shapes.

In a separate bowl, whisk the egg and a little milk for egg wash.

Roll the fishcakes in the flour, then the egg wash, then the breadcrumbs.

Fry in a deep fat fryer or frying pan until golden brown

Mix the remaining lemon and lime zest into a spoonful of mayonnaise.

Drizzle the lemon mayonnaise onto your plates with a spoonful of the tomato salad, place your warm fishcake on top and garnish with baby salad.

blue

Blue Restaurant, Cambridge Street, Edinburgh, EH1 2ED
Tel: +44 (0)131 221 1222 Fax: +44 (0)131 228 8808
Email: eat@bluescotland.co.uk www.bluescotland.co.uk

Confit of Scottish Salmon, Beetroot Jelly and Puree

By Charles Lockley, *Head Chef*, Boath House Hotel

INGREDIENTS

4 x 100g Scottish Salmon fillets. (Skin left on, scaled)

40g sea salt

20g caster sugar

5g white peppercorns (crushed)

1 lime (zest of)

½ Lemon (zest of)

½ Orange (zest of)

600g beetroot

3g agar agar

100ml port

400ml water

salt/pepper

4 x Quail eggs

100ml extra virgin oil

50ml nut oil

15ml white wine vinegar

Lemon Juice (to taste)

Chives, baby beet shoots, chervil, fennel herb

METHOD

For the salmon cure

Make sure the salmon is free of pin bones and scales and trim evenly.

Mix salt sugar, zests and peppercorns together.

Spread on plastic tray large enough to just take all the salmon. Place salmon on top of mixture flesh side down. Cover and place in fridge for 4 hours.

Peel all the beetroot and put 200g to one side.

Fine dice the remainder and put into a small pan with the water and port.

Bring to the boil and cook until soft.

Then liquidise until smooth and pass through fine sieve.

Divide this mixture into two pans. You need 200ml of beetroot puree for the jelly. Place this back into a small clean pan, add agar agar and warm for 2 minutes or until the agar has dissolved.

Pour the mixture into a cling film lined container and leave to cool.

Mix the olive, nut oil, vinegar and lemon juice together and season

Finely chop the chives and grate the remaining beetroot into a bowl. Cook Quails eggs in boiling water for 3 minutes then place in ice water to stop cooking.

Wash the salmon of its cure, pat dry then rub some olive oil over the fillet. Roll these individually in cling film making sure they are completely sealed tight.

Boath House Hotel, Auldearn, Nairn, IV12 5TE
Telephone: 01667 454896
Email: info@boath-house.com www.boath-house.com

Use a pan large enough to hold the 4 salmon pieces and half fill with water, on a low heat bring it up to 50°C, place in the fillets and warm for 15 minutes.

Remove from the water, leave to rest for a minute then carefully unwrap cling.

To assemble

Cut the jelly into cubes.

Dress the raw beetroot with the vinaigrette and chives, check seasoning.

Warm the puree, squeeze a little lemon juice on salmon.

Peel and half the quails eggs, season.

Place a pile of raw beetroot on plate, smear some puree and add jelly with half a quails egg on top (make sure all these are at room temperature).

Put salmon on raw beetroot and finish with dressed leaves and herbs.

Gratin of Tiger Prawns with Chilli and Cheese

By Seumas Macinnes, *Head Chef / Patron*, Café Gandolfi

INGREDIENTS

200g Raw tiger prawns

2-3 chopped spring onions

2 cloves crushed garlic

1 fresh red chilli, deseeded and finely chopped

280ml double cream

75g grated Gruyere cheese

juice of 1 lime

salt and pepper

METHOD

Place the prawns in a bowl with the lime juice.

At this point put your grill on its highest setting. Divide the garlic, chilli and spring onions into 4 ramekins and then place the drained prawns on top.

Season everything and top with the double cream and gruyere cheese. Put the ramekins on a baking tray and place under the grill for 5 minutes until the prawns are pink and the cheese is golden brown.

Serve with some good quality bread and perhaps a salad.

Café Gandolfi, 64 Albion Street, Glasgow, G1 1NY
Tel: 0141 552 6813 Fax: 0141 644 8911
Email: info@cafegandolfi.com www.cafegandolfi.com

'Dark Chocolate Cake with Perthshire Berries

By Ben Radford, *Head Chef* & Neil Forbes, *Head Chef*, Café St Honoré

INGREDIENTS

Makes: 1 large or 6 small cakes

400 Gram Dark Chocolate 70%

200 Gram Unsalted Butter, Diced

6 Egg Yolks

6 Eggs

200 Gram Caster Sugar

Cacao Powder

A Large Mixture of Local, Seasonal Berries, i.e. Strawberries, Raspberries, Blueberries, Brambles, Sea Buckthorn Berries

A Little Butter for Greasing

METHOD

Place chocolate and butter in a metal bowl and place over a pot of water on low heat to melt.

Meanwhile, in a large food processor or mixer, whisk the egg yolks, eggs and sugar until a pale fluffy texture .

Mix the melted chocolate and butter into the egg mix, folding lightly and spoon into either 1 large greased cake tin (non stick bottomless) or 6 small buttered cake tins.

Place into a pre heated oven for 15-20 minutes on 150-180°C until just set.

Allow to cool, but not in a fridge and remove from cake tins. You may need to use a blow torch to heat the sides of the tin.

Place onto serving plate, dust with cacao powder and serve with fresh berries.

Cafe St Honoré

Cafe St Honoré, 34 North West Thistle Street Lane, Edinburgh, EH2 1EA
Tel: +44 (0) 131 226 2211
Email: eat@cafesthonore.com www.cafesthonore.com

Roasted Saddle of Rabbit with Pancetta and Prunes and Creamed Cabbage

by Karen Mackay, *Head Chef*, Channings

INGREDIENTS

Rabbit

Serves: 1

1 saddle of rabbit

4-5 slices of pancetta

4 prunes, soaked in Armagnac

Salt and pepper

Creamed Cabbage

Serves: 4

¼ savoy cabbage, finely shredded outer leaves and white stalks removed

2 carrots julienne

1 onion, finely sliced

1clove garlic, crushed

1 sprig of thyme

25g butter

100ml double cream

Salt and pepper

METHOD

Rabbit

Pre heat your oven to 175°C, Gas Mark 3 ½.

Remove the loins of meat from the bone by feeling for the back bone and running your knife along the bone so no meat is lost. Once both of the loins are removed, place the meat flat on your chopping board, hold knife flush with the board and remove the sinew.

Lay the pancetta length ways on the chopping board side by side slightly over lapping, then place the rabbit loins about a 1/3 of the way up horizontally with the stoned prunes in between them and season.

Wrap them up folding away from you and then wrap in foil.

Place in a hot frying pan and cook for 2 minutes turning every 30 seconds or so. Roast in the oven for about 12 minutes.

Jus

Roast the rabbit bones in the oven until brown and make a stock.

Brown the scraps of the meat in a pan, add 1 glass of white wine, a splash of sherry wine vinegar and a splash of calvados, 1 bay leaf, 1 clove of garlic and a sprig of thyme.

Add rabbit or chicken stock and reduce down by 2/3.

Pass through a fine sieve, put back on to the stove and add in about 20g of butter, stirring until it dissolves. This will thicken it.

Melt the butter in a large pan then add the garlic, onion and carrots.

Sweat until almost cooked then add the cabbage and seasoning.

Cook for a minute or so then add the cream and cook down until the cabbage is cooked.

Channings, 12-16 South Learmonth Gardens, Edinburgh, EH4 1EZ
Tel: 0131 315 2226

Pan Seared Seabass with Goats Cheese Gnocchi and Apple Puree

by Craig Gibb, *Head Chef*, Cringletie House

INGREDIENTS

1 sea bass fillet cut into 4/5 pieces depending on the size.
(Use 3 pieces per portion for a starter.)

Apple Puree

1kg granny smiths, peeled and cored
100g sugar
50g butter
20g apple sours
green food colouring

Goats Cheese Gnocchi

1kg potato
350g pasta flour
4 egg yolks
100g goats cheese
parmesan
salt and pepper to taste

Goats Cheese Froth

200g milk
70g goats cheese
2g lecithin
salt

Lemon Oil

250ml lemon scented oil
250ml groundnut oil
200ml white wine vinegar
1 clove of garlic
2tsp salt
1tsp pepper

METHOD

Apple Puree

Peel and core apples then cut into even pieces.

Put the sugar in an already warm pan. When sugar is a caramel, add apples, butter and sours and cook until apples are very soft.

Blitz and add food colour until required colour pass.

Goats Cheese Gnocchi

Cook potatoes on a bed of rock salt for 2/3 hours until completely cooked. Push through sieve then dry in oven 4/5 mins.

Add yolks and cheeses and knead until smooth. Over season slightly. Add the flour and check seasoning and roll into shape.

Add to boiling water then turn down heat. Cook slowly then refresh in ice water. Dry cover in olive oil, lay on j cloths and use when required.

Goats Cheese Froth

Put goats cheese and milk into a pan and heat up 60°C. Take off heat, cling film and leave to infuse. Add lecithin then blitz. Do not heat up above 80°C when serving. Froth with hand blender.

Lemon Oil

Mix all together and put in jars. Use as needed

Garnish

Apple salad (julienne of red apple. Dress with lemon oil)
Dressed pea shoots
Lemon oil
Goats cheese froth

C
CRINGLETIE HOUSE
AN INTIMATE COUNTRY HOUSE HOTEL NEAR EDINBURGH

Cringletie House, off Edinburgh Road, Peebles, EH45 8PL
Tel: 01721 725750 Fax: 01721 725751
Email: kendal@cringletie.com www.cringletie.com

Terrine of Local Rabbit, Pigeon & Wild Mushroom with Red Pepper Chutney

By Michael Simpson, *Head Chef*, Culloden House Hotel

INGREDIENTS

For the Terrine

8 Pigeon breasts

1kg of Rabbit meat off the bone

Cabbage leaves

5 leaves of Gelatine

Salt & Pepper

250g Wild Mushrooms

1 pint of Chicken Stock

For the Red Pepper Chutney

200g of cooking apples

300g of red peppers

150g of Chopped onion

1 clove of garlic, chopped

40g of currents

60ml of White Wine vinegar

300ml of water

150g of Brown sugar

METHOD

Terrine

Boil rabbit & pigeon meat in chicken stock for 2 and a half hours, drain and leave to cool.

Sautė wild mushrooms and place on kitchen roll to drain excess moisture.

Blanch cabbage leaves.

Dissolve gelatine in half of the chicken stock.

Place cabbage leaves around terrine mould, dice the rabbit and pigeon and layer in the mould with the mushrooms, add stock/gelatine until it just covers the ingredients, place cabbage leaves over the top of ingredients and place weight onto of terrine mould, place in fridge and leave for 6 hours.

Red Pepper Chutney

Mix all ingredients with the exception of the brown sugar and bring to the boil.

Once boiling, simmer for 15 minutes

Add the brown sugar and simmer for a further hour

Remove from heat and allow to cool.

Keep in fridge.

Culloden House Hotel, Culloden, Inverness, IV2 7BZ
Telephone: +44 (0) 1463 790461 Fax: +44 (0) 1463 792181
Email: info@cullodenhouse.co.uk www.cullodenhouse.co.uk

Fruits of the Sea for Two

By Roy Brett, *Chef Partner*, Dakota Hotels

INGREDIENTS

1 Scottish Lobster (cooked)

1 Scottish Crab (cooked)

4 Langoustines

1 handful of mussels

1 handful of cockles

1 handful of clams

1 lemon

METHOD

To prepare the lobster split the lobster in half, length ways. Simply remove the digestive track that lies along tail. Break off the claws and crack open.

To prepare the crab break off the claws and crack open.

Turn the crab on its back and press the body section up until it comes apart. Pull out the gills or the feathery looking things. Split the body in half then set aside, placing the top shell back on.

To prepare the langoustines cook the prawns in boiling salted water, as soon as they float to the top they are ready. Set aside.

In a small steamer place the mussels, clams and cockles inside and steam for ten to twenty seconds or until the shells lightly open, then remove and set aside.

To open the oysters, simply press your knife into the hinge of the oyster slipping the knife along the shell avoiding spilling any of the beautiful juices.

To assemble crush a bag of ice and pour into a deep dish.

Arrange the shellfish in any way you like trying to give the prime shells in the centre of the dish. Garnish with a little edible seaweed and lemon wedges.

Serve with some good quality sourdough and mayonnaise.

Scottish Restaurant of the Year 2008

Scottish Hotel Restaurant of the Year 2008

Dakota Forth Bridge, Queensferry, Edinburgh, EH30 9QZ
Tel: 0870 423 4293 Fax: 0131 319 3699
www.dakotahotels.co.uk

Baileys, Chocolate and Malteser Cheesecake

by James Mackenzie, *Head Chef / Proprietor*, Digby Chick

INGREDIENTS

200g cream cheese

3 heaped tbsp icing sugar

200ml double cream

100g melted plain chocolate, 50% cocoa solids or higher

Packet of Maltesers

100ml Baileys

50g melted butter

200g chocolate digestives

METHOD

Mix together crushed digestives and melted butter and press into a springform tin and chill.

Beat until smooth the cream cheese and icing sugar.

Then add the double cream and Baileys and beat until it reaches a dropping consistency. Don't let it thicken too much.

Now spread half of this onto your chilled biscuit base and push the Maltesers into the mixture.

Add the melted dark chocolate in to the remaining half of your mixture and stir gently. Cover the cheesecake with this to create two layers and chill for 2 hours.

Serve with lots more Baileys if you like!

Digby Chick, 5 Bank Street, Stornoway, Isle of Lewis, HS1 2XG
Tel: 01851 70 0026

Tian of West Coast Crab with Brioche Toasts

by Phil McDonald, *Head Chef / Patron*, Dine

INGREDIENTS

Serves: 4

Crab mix

250g white crab meat, checked for shell and cartilage

1 granny smith apple, peeled, cored and finely diced

½ ripe but firm avocado, finely diced

Juice of 2 lemons and zest of one, finely chopped

Sea salt and freshly ground pepper

2tbsp mayonnaise (ready made is fine)

2tbsp full fat crème fraîche

Garnish

4 slices of brioche loaf (slowly toasted)

Baby pea shoots

Balsamic vinegar (reduced)

METHOD

Gently fold all of the ingredients together in a bowl.

Place a pastry cutter in the centre of a serving plate.

Spoon the crab mixture into the ring and fill to the top.

Press down with the back of the spoon to level it off.

Carefully remove the ring and repeat the process for the other portions.

Arrange the brioche toast and pea shoots on top of the crab tian and garnish with a little of the balsamic reduction.

Dine, 205, Fenwick Rd, Giffnock, Glasgow, G46 6JD
Tel: 0141 621 1903
Email info@dinegiffnock.co.uk www.dinegiffnock.co.uk

Broken Lemon Tart

by Mark Greenaway, *Head Chef*, Dryburgh Abbey Hotel

INGREDIENTS

Garnish

280g yuzu juice

280g sugar

280g whole eggs

350g butter

6 sheets Gelatine (soaked in enough water to cover)

Shortbread

900g Plain Flour

600g Butter (unsalted)

300g Caster sugar

Pistachio purée

850g pistachios

325mls pistachio oil

200g sugar

10g salt

500g water

200g glucose

Coconut Jelly

250mls milk

250 coconut cream

80g caster sugar

4 sheets of gelatine (soaked in enough water to cover)

4 Pieces of frozen watermelon 1cm square

METHOD

Yuzu Curd Jelly

Place the yuzu juice in a saucepan and bring to a boil. Meanwhile, combine the eggs and sugar in a bowl and beat with a whip to combine. Add the yuzu juice into the egg mixture and return to the saucepan. Bring to a 82°C while stirring constantly. Add softened gelatine. Transfer the mixture to a blender and blend on low speed. Add the butter little by little until it is all incorporated. Pour the mixture into a plastic cling filmed tray and allow to gel in the refrigerator. Slice the gel into 1 ½cm squares using a sharp knife

Shortbread

Combine all the ingredients in a food processor and pulse until the butter is no longer visible. Spread the mixture evenly across a parchment-lined tray and bake in an oven at 180°C until deep brown. Allow the mixture to cool. Return the mixture to a food processor and purée until a stiff paste is achieved. Roll the mixture to a 1/4-inch thickness between two sheets of greaseproof paper. Cut the shortbread into 1-1/2-inch squares. Store in freezer until required.

Pistachio Purée

Combine all the ingredients in a blender and purée until smooth. Pass through a fine sieve and refrigerate in an airtight container.

Coconut Jelly

Bring all ingredients to the simmer and add the softened gelatine. Set in a cling filmed lined tray.

To Finish the Dish

Arrange 4 pieces of the yuzu curd and shortbread on the plate and 4 pieces of frozen watermelon, Cut and place coconut jelly in centre of plate, Place some Drops of pistachio purée and yuzu Curd on the plate. Serve.

Yuzu curd: (thin down some of the yuzu jelly with a dash of cream), we also serve it with yuzu ice cream tube (in picture)

Basil Panna Cotta with Mascarpone Ravioli and a Blood Orange Sauce

by Paul Moffat, *Head Chef*, Enterkine Country House

NGREDIENTS

asil Panna Cotta

00mls double cream
0g caster sugar
leaves of fresh basil
½ leaves of bronze gelatine

avioli

Vhole fresh pineapple
lemon
orange
00mls water
0g caster sugar
bay leaves
cinnamon stick
cardoman pod
5g mascarpone cheese
00g fresh wild strawberries

lood Orange Sauce

blood oranges
00mls fresh orange juice
0g caster sugar
tsp arrow root

METHOD

Basil Panna Cotta

Soak the gelatine in cold water until soft.

Add sugar to the cream and the soft gelatine then bring to the boil to dissolve the sugar.

Let the cream cool to about 50°C and add the basil leaves. Blend with a hand blender and leave to infuse for 10mins.

Strain the mixture into Dario moulds or timbales.

Place into the fridge to set completely (usually takes about 1 hour).

Ravioli

Place 300mls of water, 2 lemon wedges, 2 orange wedges, 2 bay leaves, 1 cinnamon stick and 1 cardoman pod into a heavy pan and boil with 50g of caster sugar for about 10 mins. Take off the heat and allow to cool.

Very thinly slice the peeled pineapple (on a meat slicer if possible) and place the slices into the syrup mix to marinade.

Mix some diced strawberries with the mascarpone cheese and place into a piping bag then take 2 slices of the pineapple and pipe some of the cheese onto the pasta disc.

Fold over into a half moon shape. Serve 2 ravioli as a portion.

Blood Orange Sauce

Segment the blood orange and place in a pan with the orange juice and sugar.

Simmer for about 15mins and blend with a stick blender.

Mix 1tsp of arrow root with water and thicken the sauce slightly and allow to cool before serving.

Enterkine

Enterkine Country House, Annbank, by Ayr, KA6 5AL
Tel: 01292 520580 Fax: 01292 521582
Email: mail@enterkine.com www.enterkine.com

Fish Soup with Crab Meat, Stem Ginger and Coriander

By Derek Marshall, *Head Chef*, Gamba

INGREDIENTS

275g white fish meat (haddock, cod or whiting)

4 cloves of garlic

50g root ginger

2 medium onions, chopped

50g unsalted butter

3 tbsp. plain flour

1.15 lt. fish stock

1 packet of coriander

50g grated stem ginger

3 tbsp. tomato puree

450g white crabmeat

75ml brandy

METHOD

Melt the butter over a low heat in a thick-bottomed pan.

Chop the onions, garlic and root ginger and sweat in a covered pan with the butter. Add brandy and reduce.

Mix in the flour and cook for about five minutes, still on a low heat.

Add the tomato puree and keep mixing. Start adding fish stock little by little, mixing all the time.

Add the white fish meat and cook for 30 to 40 minutes.

Liquidise the soup and pass through a sieve into a clean pot or bowl.

Add the crabmeat, grated stem ginger and chopped coriander.

Serve in warm soup bowls with garlic bread.

Gamba, 225a West George Street, Glasgow, G2 2ND
Tel: 0141 572 0899 Fax: 0141 572 0896
www.gamba.co.uk

Roasted Sea Bass with Cockles

with a Fennel and Vanilla Salad and a Fennel and Dill Purée

By Adam Stokes, *Head Chef*, Glenapp Castle

INGREDIENTS

Serves: 8

Sea Bass & Cockles

2kg Wild Line Caught Sea Bass (scaled and filleted into 8 portions)

30 Cockles

100g Sauternes Sweet Wine

Olive Oil

Butter

Fennel & Vanilla Salad

1 Bulb of Fennel

2 Vanilla Pods

50ml Grapeseed Oil

Fennel & Dill Purée

1 Bulb of Fennel – finely sliced

300g Water

15g Pernod

50ml Double Cream

Chopped Dill

To Season

Lemon

Salt

METHOD

I love this beautifully simple dish. It showcases Scotland's fantastic fish and seafood. To capture the true magic of this dish you will need the freshest line caught wild sea bass and beautifully fresh plump cockles.

Fennel & Vanilla Salad

Vanilla Oil - marinade the vanilla pods in grapeseed oil and leave in a warm place for 24 hours.

30 minutes before serving, slice the fennel on a mandolin and season with salt, lemon and vanilla oil. Leave to soften in a warm place for 20 minutes. Save some vanilla oil to glaze the fish at the end.

Fennel & Dill Purée

Place the finely sliced bulb of fennel in a pan with the water and Pernod, boil until soft (approximately 15 minutes) and strain – keep this cooking liquid. Put the softened fennel and double cream into a food blender and blend whilst gradually adding the cooking liquid until a smooth purée is produced. Finally, add the dill.

Sea Bass & Cockles

Heat the olive oil in a non-stick pan, sear the fillets of sea bass and season with salt and a squeeze of lemon. Finish with a knob of butter and glaze with vanilla oil. Place the cockles and Sauternes in a hot pan and cook until the cockles open (approximately 1 minute) at which point season with salt and lemon.

To Serve

Place the fennel and vanilla salad in a small heap slightly off centre on the plate. Add the sea bass on top (skin side up). For the tear drop of fennel and dill purée, put a spoonful of purée onto the plate and drag the back of a spoon through the spoonful. Dress the dish with the cockles, glaze the top of the sea bass with vanilla oil and drizzle a little vanilla oil over the plate.

Roast Fennel, Aubergine & Mushrooms with a Fennel Sauce & Pecorino Cheese

by Guy Cowan, *Head Chef / Patron*, Guy's Restaurant and Bar

INGREDIENTS

1 head fennel.

1 aubergine.

4 medium sized mushrooms, any variety but porcini work best.

Pecorino cheese (or fresh Parmesan) grated. If for vegetarians, there are cheeses made with vegetable rennet available.

Virgin olive oil.

Chicken or vegetable stock. (Chicken is best but if you are feeding vegetarians use vegetable stock).

1 measure of Pernod or Pastis.

1/2 cup double cream (use crème fraîche or natural yoghurt if you feel like being healthy).

Malden salt & freshly ground black pepper.

Finely chopped parsley.

White truffle oil (optional).

METHOD

Slice the aubergine in 0.5cm thick 'rings', lay on a tray a sprinkle quite liberally with salt. Leave for about 30 minutes, this will draw out the bitter juices. Rinse well under running cold water then pat dry. Brush with olive oil and sear on a hot griddle pan on both sides until cooked, again be careful not to burn the vegetable. If you do not have a griddle pan then grill them or oven roast remembering to turn them over once. Leave to cool.

After salting the aubergine prepare fennel; cut widthways into 'rings' about 0.75cm, toss in olive oil to coat and place on a tray in hot oven. Roast, turning once until cooked through, about 10/15 minutes but do not let burn. Take out and leave to cool.

Clean mushrooms with a damp cloth, not in water, and slice about 1cm thick.

Reduce about a cup of stock by half then add double cream and continue to simmer until the liquid thickens and coats the back of a spoon.

Take about one third of the roast fennel, blitz in a processor and add to the reduction of the stock and double cream.

Add Pernod, adjust seasoning, cook for another couple of minutes then leave to cool.

Using a metal ring, 7cm diameter, put a layer of fennel, a little sauce, aubergine, another spoon of sauce, mushroom and more sauce. Lightly season each level. Repeat the process and top with the grated cheese. Put on the middle shelf of a hot oven for approximately 12/15 minutes being careful not to burn. Take out and put on plate being careful when removing metal ring.

Drizzle with truffle oil, sprinkle with parsley, and serve with a little mizuna or rocket salad.

Any left over vegetables can be dressed with olive oil, balsamic vinegar and used as a salad, mixed with remaining fennel sauce and served with penne or rigatoni or put on a sandwich with cheese, parma ham, salami, chicken or whatever you wish.

Guy's Restaurant & Bar, 24 Candleriggs, Merchant City, Glasgow, G1 1LD
Tel: 0141 552 1114 Fax: 0141 552 3718
Email: info@guysrestaurant.co.uk www.guysrestaurant.co.uk

Fillets Of Sea Bass wrapped around a Seafood Mousse

by Paul Lumby, *Head Chef*, The Harbour Inn

INGREDIENTS

Serves: 8

Cooking time: 20 minutes

4 whole sea bass (250-300g) filleted

For the seafood mousse

750g of sole, salmon and prawns

2 large eggs

Fresh tarragon, finely chopped

200ml double cream

Freshly ground salt and black pepper

For the puree

1 small head of celeriac, peeled and diced

50ml double cream

20g butter

1tsp of chopped truffle (or 1tsp good quality truffle oil can be substituted)

For garnish

8 King Scallops

Garden herb dressing

Balsamic glaze

METHOD

Set the oven at 180°C.

First make the mousse; ensure all skin and bones are removed from the fish and transfer the fish to a food processor. Add the eggs and process until smooth. Season and add the fresh tarragon and cream and mix to a smooth puree.

Lay one sea bass fillet flat; put a small amount of mousse over the fillet and roll the sea bass fillet around it. Secure with a fine wooden skewer/cocktail stick. Place mousse-down on an oiled baking tray and bake for 20 minutes.

Meanwhile, cook the celeriac in simmering salted water until soft. This will take around 10 minutes. Drain and mash to a puree then add the cream, butter and truffle/oil. Keep warm. Swiftly sear the scallops and also keep warm.

To serve

Place the celeriac in a ring mould in the centre of your plate. Remove mould and put one of the sea bass fillets on top. Garnish with pan-fried scallops, drizzle with the herb dressing and balsamic glaze and fresh tarragon.

The Harbour Inn and Restaurant, Bowmore, Isle of Islay, Argyll, PA43 7JR
Tel: 01496 810330 Fax: 01496 810990
Email: info@harbour-inn.com www.harbour-inn.com

Scottish Blue Lobster, Cauliflower Salad and Yoghurt Beignets

by Matthew Gray, *Executive Chef*, Inverlochy Castle Hotel and Restaurant

INGREDIENTS

Lobster

1 x 800g lobster cooked (for 2 persons)

Cauliflower salad

cooked cauliflower florets

1 tomato concasse (peeled, seeded and diced)

chopped chives

French Vinaigrette

1 egg yolk

100ml balsamic

75ml raspberry vinegar

(1) 60ml sherry vinegar
    2½g salt
    5g sugar
    8g Dijon mustard

(2) 300g ground nut oil

(3) 250g cream

(4) 1 clove of garlic
    Rosemary
    Basil

3tbsp french dressing

1tbsp crème fraîche

Yoghurt Beignet

250g good quality natural yoghurt

tabasco to taste

dried bread crumbs

salt and pepper

METHOD

Hang the yoghurt in muslin overnight to remove excess moisture.

Season with salt, pepper and Tabasco. Roll into balls and breadcrumb.

Remove shell from lobster and cut into desired size.

Make the dressing by mixing the ingredients together in the above order i.e. 1,2,3 & 4.

Add crème fraîche to dressing base before using.

Assembly

Mix the cauliflower, concasse, chives and vinaigrette together. Season to taste.

Deep fry beignets until golden then season.

Place salad on the plate and neatly arrange the lobster and beignets on top.

Garnish with chervil. Extra dressing can be put on plate if desired.

INVERLOCHY CASTLE
Hotel & Restaurant

Inverlochy Castle Hotel, Torlundy, Fort William, PH33 6SN
Tel: +44 (0) 1397 702177 Fax: +44 (0) 1397 702953
www.inverlochycastlehotel.com

Roast Loin of Highland Roe Deer

with Sweet and Sour Beetroot, Haggis Beignet, Pomme Anna and a Juniper and Port Reduction

By Tony Pierce, *Head Chef*, Knockinaam Lodge

INGREDIENTS

Serves: 4

1 loin of Highland Roe Deer (trimmed)

4oz of Haggis

2 Maris Piper Potatoes

1 Beetroot (peeled and cut into 1 inch cubes)

Beer Batter

4 Confit Shallots

8 Baby Carrots

4 tbsp Smooth Parsnip Puree

Sauce

2 fl oz of Water

8 fl oz of Chicken Stock

2 fl oz of Veal Stock

2 oz of Roe Deer Bones

4 oz of Root Vegetables Diced (Shallot, Carrot, Celery, Leek)

1 fl oz of Raspberry Vinegar

4 fl oz of Port

4 Juniper Berries

Half an ounce of Butter

Sprig of Thyme

METHOD

Beetroot

Place the beetroot in a pan with 1 fl oz of Red Wine Vinegar, 1 fl oz of Port, teaspoon of Redcurrant Jelly, a little Orange Zest and Water. Cook for approx. 40 minutes on a low heat, keep warm.

Pomme Anna

Slice Potatoes and place in an overlapping layer in a small pan with clarified Butter. Cook until golden brown on one side. Turn and repeat.

Juniper Sauce

Caramelise bones in heavy bottomed sauce pan for approx. 6 minutes then add root vegetables and sweat for approx. 4 minutes, add juniper berries, thyme and raspberry vinegar, evaporate then add half the port, evaporate and add all stock and water, simmer for approx. 30 minutes, pass through muslin cloth into a new pan with the remainder of the port and reduce by two thirds. Finish with butter. Keep warm.

Roe Deer

Season, sear and cook the Roe Deer in a frying pan basting continually for approx. 4 minutes, rest for 10 minutes, keep warm.

Haggis Beignet

Divide haggis into four, shape into balls, flour, beer batter and deep fry until golden brown approx. 2 minutes.

Parsnip Puree

1 parsnip boiled and pureed with 2oz of best butter. Keep warm.

Serve and enjoy!!

***Tony Pierce** was awarded "Chef of the Year 2008"*

Knockinaam Lodge

Knockinaam Lodge, Portpatrick, Dumfries and Galloway, DG9 9AD
Tel: 01776 810471 Fax: 01776 810435
Email: reservations@knockinaamlodge.com www.knockinaamlodge.com

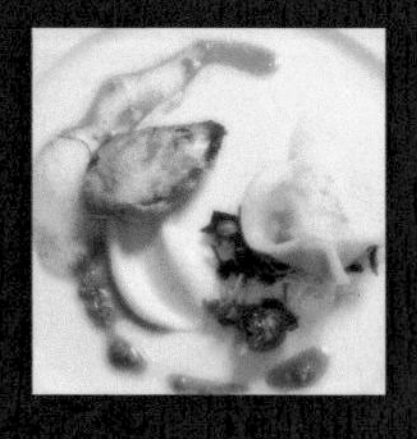

Pan Seared Breast of Mr Byrnes Partridge *with a Ravioli of its Leg*

By Daniel Hollern, *Head Chef*, The Linen Room

INGREDIENTS

2 whole partridges

Chopped herbs

Pasta

8oz '00' pasta flour

2 egg yolks

2 whole eggs

10mls olive oil

Chervil root purée

500g-chervil root

Milk to cover

100g butter

Salt and white pepper

Nut of garlic

Oat foam

170g oats, toasted until golden and fragrant

1 litre milk

175 ml water

15g salt

5g lecithin

Selection of baby leaves.

METHOD

Partridge

Take the breast from the partridge and set aside. De-bone the legs, take skin off and chop finely. Add a small amount of chopped herbs for colour and set aside as filling for raviolis.

Pasta

Combine all the ingredients into a standard kitchen blender, and set on blend until it forms dough. Carefully take out and make sure it's in an even dough. Leave this to set in the fridge for a minimum of twenty minutes. Meantime, set up your pasta machine. Once the pasta is ready to work, take out and pass through your pasta machine until the required thickness. Lay the sheet of pasta down and cut two required shapes (you will need 8 of the same shapes minimum). Put a generous amount of leg mix in the centre and then lightly wet around the edge, lay one round over and shape into a ravioli and trim up edges neatly. Set aside on lightly floured tray until finishing the dish.

Oat foam

Toast your oats until fragrant and add to milk and water. Leave it to infuse for ten minutes minimum and pass through a fine chinois, blend in the lecithin and salt and set aside for use.

Chervil root purée (this can be any good root vegetable)

Peel the chervil root and cut to roughly the same size, put in pot with the nut of garlic and cover with milk. Let simmer (not boil) on the stove until soft, take off and strain but retain the cooking liquor. Put the drained root

the linen room

The Linen Room, 53 St. Michael Street, Dumfries, DG1 2QB
Tel: 01387 255689
Email: linenroom@yahoo.co.uk www.linenroom.com

into a stand up blender and put on high speed. Slowly add some of the cooking liquor and butter and blend until smooth. Add seasoning to taste.

Finishing the dish

In pots, gently heat up the purée and the oat foam separately (do not boil). Have a pot of salted water boiling for the ravioli and bring up to heat a frying pan for the breasts of partridge. Colour the presentation side of the partridge and turn and take off the heat. Drop the ravioli into the boiling water for three to five minutes.

On a plate, put a generous spoon of purée in the centre and drag spoon through it. Dress small amount of salad leaves and put on plate, take out ravioli and drain and season and place on top of leaves. Place breast on top of purée and using a hand blender, gently foam the oat foam until its bubbly and scoop bubbles on to top of the ravioli.

Serve immediately.

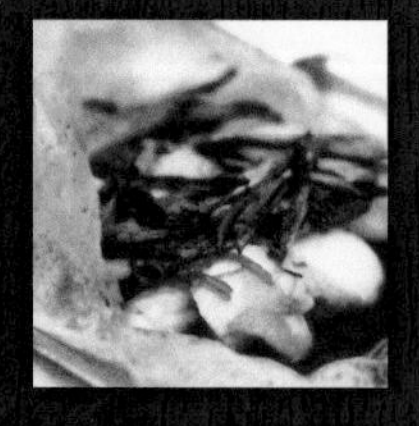

Scallops and Monkfish en Papillotte

By Jim Kerr, *Executive Chef*, Mar Hall Hotel

INGREDIENTS

8 pieces of greaseproof paper cut to size of your plate

16 scallops

2 monkfish tail cut into 16 pieces

8 spring onions

60g fresh root ginger

1 tsp Demerara sugar

juice of 1 lemon

2 tbsp sweet soya sauce

METHOD

Lightly grease the paper with oil.

Sweat ginger in a little oil on the stove, add brown sugar and stir, add lemon juice and sweet soya. Take off gas and mix in spring onions, do not cook.

Place scallops and monkfish alternately on piece of greaseproof paper season with salt.

Sprinkle ginger and spring onion mix on top with a little juice.

Place another piece of greaseproof paper on top and fold sides in order to overlap tightly.

Cook in oven on greased tray at gas mark 8 until greaseproof paper rises, which indicates that the fish is cooked.

Serve straight out of the oven as the fish will continue to cook in the paper.

This is a very quick way to cook fish.

Mar Hall Hotel, Earl of Mar Estate, Bishopton, Nr Glasgow, PA7 5NW
Tel: 0141 812 9999 Fax: 0141 812 9997
Email: sales@marhall.com www.marhall.com

Slow Braised Shin and Cutlet of Grampian Lamb *with Barley Risotto and Wilted Wild Garlic*

by Neil Rae, *Proprietor*, The Milton

INGREDIENTS

9 pieces lamb shin
1 rack lamb
seasoned flour
200g mirepoix (carrot, celery, onion)
2 glasses red wine
bouquet garni
1 ltr lamb stock
1 tbsp tomato puree
salt and pepper

Barley Risotto

2 large shallots
1 clove garlic
1 glass white wine
20g butter
½ pt chicken stock
2 tbsp grated parmesan
50 ml double cream
200g pearl barley (soaked in cold water overnight)

Wilted Wild Garlic

400g wild garlic
20g butter

METHOD

Lightly coat lamb shin in flour and brown in a hot pan with a little oil. Remove from pan and set aside.

Add mirepoix to same pan and brown. Add tomato puree and deglaze with red wine. Add lamb shins, stock and bouquet garni.

Cover and braise for 1-1½ hours or until tender

Remove the meat from the pan and reduce the braising liquid. Return shins to stock and keep warm.

French trim the rack of lamb, remove the membrane and score the fat.

Season and seal well in a hot pan. Move to a hot oven for 7-8 mins. Remove and rest. Slice before serving.

Barley Risotto

Sweat chopped shallots and garlic in butter, add barley and sweat. Add white wine and reduce heat. Add the stock a little at a time until the barley is 'al dente', stir in cream, season and add parmesan. Keep warm.

Wilted Wild Garlic

Wilt garlic leaves in a hot pan with the butter and season.

the milton restaurant

The Milton, Crathes, Banchory, Aberdeenshire
Tel: 01330 844566
Email: jan@themilton.co.uk www.themilton.co.uk

Composition of Mosside Pork Roast Fillet of Pork, Braised Pork Belly and Pork Faggot

INGREDIENTS

For the Pork Fillet

1 x 500g pork fillet
10 rashers of pancetta
250g pork trimmings
125ml whipping cream
zest of ½ lemon
thyme leaves
1 egg white
salt and pepper
soft butter

For the Pork Belly

500g pork belly, rind on
1 cinnamon stick
2 star-anise
25g piece of root ginger, grated
2 bay leaves
Sprig of thyme
Pinch black pepper corns
4 cloves garlic, crushed
400ml dark soya sauce
100ml sweet chilli sauce
1 pt water

METHOD

Pork Fillet

Trim and remove all sinew. Cut away top and tail and use this for your mousse. Blitz the trimmings in a robot coupe, add the egg white and cream until smooth. Place mousse into a bowl, mix in lemon zest, thyme leaves and lightly season.

Lightly butter a sheet of tin foil and lay out pancetta overlapping each rasher. Spread on a thin layer of mousse and place the pork fillet on top, season and wrap the pork fillet pulling it towards you. Twist the ends of the tin foil to make a tight log shape. Leave to rest in fridge.

Pork Belly

First braise the pork. Lightly season the pork and combine all ingredients, place in a deep roasting tin and cover with foil. If the cooking stock does not cover the pork add more water.

Cook in oven at 130°C for 4 hours or until pork is tender. Remove the pork from oven. Lay a sheet of parchment paper over pork and place another tray on top to press down the pork belly. Weigh down the pork and leave to press in fridge overnight.

A member of Small Luxury Hotels of the World and Connoisseurs Scotland

Marcliffe Hotel and Spa, North Deeside Road, Pitfodels, Aberdeen AB15 9YA
Tel: 01224 861000 Fax: 01224 868860
Email: enquiries@marcliffe.com www.marcliffe.com

by Colin Rennie, *Sous Chef* and Ross Spence, *Sous Chef*, The Marcliffe Hotel, Spa And Restaurant

INGREDIENTS

For the Pork Faggot

4 shallots, chopped
4oz pancetta, diced
6oz pork shoulder, diced
2oz bread crumbs
½tsp chopped parsley
1 whole egg
500ml veal stock

For the Fondant Potato

2 large baking potatoes
sprig of thyme
1 bay leaf
500ml chicken stock
100g butter

For the Artichoke Puree

200g peeled Jerusalem artichokes

For the Vegetable Garnish

12 asparagus spears, fully trimmed
mixed wild mushrooms

METHOD

Pork Faggot

Sweat off the shallots, pancetta and pork shoulder. Mince through a fine mincer and add the parsley combining the egg and bread crumbs. If the mix becomes too dry add a little veal stock. Shape the mix into balls and place on a buttered roasting tin, add the veal stock and cook for 1 hour at 180°C.

Fondant Potato

Cut off the flat edges and punch out rounds using a pastry cutter. Seal off in a hot pan with some butter until golden brown, place in a small roasting tin with the herbs and enough stock to cover the potato by ¾. Cook in the oven at 170°C for 40minutes or until cooked.

Artichoke puree

Boil artichokes in a pan with ½ water and ½ milk until tender then drain and puree with blender. Keep hot.

Vegetable Garnish

Prepare and sauté the vegetable garnish.

When ready to serve, roast off the pork fillet for 30 minutes. While this is in the oven, remove the rind from the belly and cut into portions. Reheat in small saucepan using the cooking stock.

To serve, divide all ingredients onto 4 plates and arrange as desired.

Wild Salmon with Lentils and Bacon Tomato Butter Sauce

by Craig Millar, *Head Chef / Patron*, The Seafood Restaurant

INGREDIENTS

Serves: 4

4 x 150g Fillets of Wild Salmon (de-scaled)
150g Puy lentils (soaked for 1 hour)
2 carrots
1 shallot
1 Bay leaf
1 tbsp olive oil
50g smoked bacon, cut into lardons
2 tbsp vinaigrette
salt and pepper

Sauce

250g vine-ripened tomatoes
1 tbsp Sherry vinegar
1 tbsp caster sugar
1 tbsp chopped fresh basil
100ml double cream
50g butter (diced)

METHOD

Make The Sauce

Halve the tomatoes then blend with vinegar, sugar and basil in a food processor. Pass through a sieve into a saucepan, reduce by half and whisk in the butter. Season with salt and pepper.

Lentils

Drain the lentils and place into a saucepan with one of the carrots, half the leek, half the shallot and Bay leaf and cover with cold water. Bring to the boil and simmer for 20 mins (until lentils are soft). Drain and discard the vegetables and Bay leaf.

Finally chop the remaining vegetables, heat the oil in a saucepan and add the bacon and vegetables. Cook until soft and season. Add lentils and vinaigrette

Cook The Salmon

Place the Salmon in a hot non-stick pan skin side down, add the oil and season. Cook for 2-3 mins then turn over for additional 2-3 mins.

Serving

Spoon the lentils into the middle of a warmed plate, top with salmon and spoon sauce around.

The Seafood Restaurant, Bruce Embankment, St Andrews, Fife
Tel: 01334 479 475 Fax: 01334 479 476
Email: standrews@theseafoodrestaurant.com www.theseafoodrestaurant.com

Red Tuna Steak with Nicoise Salad Vegetables

By Didier Dejean, Silver Darling Seafood Restaurant

INGREDIENTS

Nicoise salad

2 tomatoes
½ cucumber
½ red bell pepper
100g fresh green beans
3 pink radishes
200g small fava beans
20 black olives
12 basil leaves
½ cos lettuce
2 spring onions
2 fillets salted anchovies
3 thin slices slow roast tomatoes
2 tablespoons basil oil
Fleur de sel
Freshly ground pepper
Espelette chilli

Red Tuna

4 slices (200g each) of red tuna
balsamic vinegar
15mls olive oil

METHOD

Cut tomatoes into quarters and remove seeds, keeping only the flesh.

Peel the cucumber, remove the seeds and use a vegetable peeler to cut into ribbons.

Peel the red bell pepper and cut into cubes.

Boil the green beans in salted water.

Finely slice the pink radishes and spring onions.

Combine all the vegetables and season with olive oil, basil oil, fleur de sel and freshly ground pepper.

Set aside in the fridge.

Marinate the tuna steak in balsamic vinegar for 5 minutes.

Blot dry and sprinkle with espelette chilli.

Sauté the tuna in a little olive oil (30 seconds on each side) and transfer to serving dish.

Arrange the vegetables attractively on the tuna with the anchovy fillets and olives.

Use the rest of the balsamic marinade together with the basil oil as dressing and sprinkle with fleur de sel.

Silver Darling Seafood Restaurant, Pocra Quay, North Pier, Aberdeen, AB11 5DQ
Tel: 01224 576229 Fax: 01224 588119
www.silverdarlingrestaurant.co.uk

Puff Candy Meringue

by Jacqueline O'Donnell, *Chef / Patron*, The Sisters

INGREDIENTS

Serves: 6-8

Meringue

4 egg whites

100g caster sugar

Puff Candy (or buy a Crunchie)

½ lb sugar

2 ½ tbsp golden syrup

2 ½ tbsp bicarbonate of soda

Butterscotch Sauce

100g sugar

100g butter

100ml double cream

METHOD

Meringue

Whisk and add sugar gradually to form soft peaks. You can also fold some crushed puff candy through before baking. Spoon mixture onto greaseproof paper about 6cm diametre and bake for 40mins at 150°C/Gas Mark 3. You still want it to be chewy in the middle.

Puff Candy

Boil sugar & syrup together until light golden& remove from the heat.

Stir soda in quickly until frothy and pour into greased tray, leave to cool.

Butterscotch Sauce

Boil the sugar & butter until dark golden brown then carefully add double cream. Simmer for 2 minutes. Use a high sided pot as this mixture will boil up quite high. Store in a jar in the fridge.

This will keep in the fridge for 3-4wks...if you can keep it there for that length of time.

Once the meringues are ready, spoon a good quality ice-cream in the centre, sprinkle with crushed Puff candy & heat 1 tbsp per portion of sauce and pour over the top.

The Sisters

The Sisters, 36 Kelvingrove Street, Kelvingrove, Glasgow G3 7RZ
Tel: 0141 564 1157
Email: info@thesisters.co.uk www.thesisters.co.uk

Lightly Fried Aromatic Duck Egg, Ham Mousse and Pea Shoots

by Graeme Pallister, *Chef / Patron*, 63 Tay Street

NGREDIENTS

Ham mousse

200g finest cooked ham, finely diced
200g white roux, lightly seasoned
00ml lightly whipped cream
sheet of gelatine
Sherry
Paprika
Cayenne Pepper
Salt

omato vinaigrette

ripe tomato, skinned, deseeded nd diced
red chilli, blackened, skinned and nely diced
½ red pepper, blackened, skinned nd finely diced
teaspoon of salted capers, rinsed nd dried
tablespoons of quality olive oil
dessertspoonful of cabernet auvignon vinegar

o serve

duck eggs
tablespoons of clarified butter
0g fresh pea shoots
selection of equal quantities of oasted spice seeds
teaspoon of a vanilla sugar syrup r maple syrup

METHOD

Ham Mousse

Soften gelatine in cold water, squeeze and dissolve in 2 tablespoons of warm sherry. In a blender place ham, roux and gelatine and blend until smooth. Remove to a bowl and gently fold in cream and season to taste with sherry, paprika, salt and the cayenne. Leave to set in fridge for at least 2 hours.

Tomato Vinaigrette

Combine all ingredients, season to taste, reserve.

To Serve

Warm the butter in a non-stick pan and cook egg to your liking. Lightly season once cooked and place on a warmed plate, add vinaigrette to egg, seeds and dot of syrup on yolk, quenelle of ham mousse with hot spoons and top with peas shoots, serve immediately.

63 Tay Street Restaurant, Perth, PH2 8NN
Tel: 01738 441451 Fax: 01738 441461
Email: info@63taystreet.com www.63taystreet.com

The Three Chimneys Famous Hot Marmalade Pudding

by Shirley Spear, The Three Chimneys

INGREDIENTS

150g fine brown breadcrumbs

120g soft brown sugar

25g self-raising wholemeal flour (white self-raising would do)

120g fresh butter, plus extra for greasing the bowl

8 tbsp well-flavoured, coarse-cut marmalade (homemade is always the best)

3 large eggs

1 rounded tsp bicarbonate of soda plus water to mix

Drambuie Custard

275mls fresh milk

275mls fresh double cream

6 egg yolks

100g caster sugar

2 tbsp Drambuie liqueur

METHOD

Butter a 3-pint pudding basin well.

Place the breadcrumbs, flour and sugar in a large mixing bowl.

Melt the butter together with the marmalade in a saucepan over a gentle heat. Pour the melted ingredients over the dry ingredients and mix together thoroughly.

Whisk the eggs until frothy and beat gently into the mixture until blended together well.

Last of all, dissolve the bicarbonate of soda in a tbsp of cold water. Stir this into the pudding mixture which will increase in volume as it absorbs the bicarbonate of soda.

Spoon the mixture into the prepared basin. Cover it with close-fitting lid or alternatively make a lid of circles of buttered greaseproof paper and foil, pleated together across the centre and tie securely around the rim of the basin.

Place the pudding basin in a saucepan of boiling water. The water should reach halfway up the side of the basin. Cover the pan with a close-fitting lid and simmer the pudding for 2 hours. The water will need topping up throughout the cooking period. Turn out on to a serving dish. Slice and serve hot with fresh cream, ice cream or – as we do at Three Chimneys – with Drambuie Custard.

the three chimneys

THE RESTAURANT
THE HOUSE OVER-BY

The Three Chimneys, Colbost, Dunvegan, Isle of Skye, IV55 8ZT
Tel: 01470 511258 Fax: 01470 511358
Email: eatandstay@threechimneys.co.uk www.threechimneys.co.uk

Drambuie Custard

This is a proper egg custard flavoured with Drambuie liqueur. It is served warm, poured around the pudding. Alternative flavours could be added such as vanilla, ginger or crushed cardamon, if you prefer. A tablespoonful of fresh ground coffee can be added which is delicious with hot or cold chocolate desserts.

Whisk the egg yolks together with the sugar until pale, slightly thick and creamy.

Gently warm the milk and cream until it is just beginning to bubble.

Pour the milk and cream on to the egg and sugar mixture and whisk together.

Return the mixture to the saucepan.

Bring to the boil very slowly, stirring all the time. As soon as it begins to thickens, or coats the back of the wooden spoon, remove from the heat and pour into a bowl or jug for serving.

Stir in the Drambuie, or flavouring of your choice.

Serve immediately. Alternatively, cool the custard quickly in a bowl sitting on ice and refrigerate when cold until required. The custard can be used cold for assembling a trifle, serving with frozen or chilled desserts or reheated carefully for serving with a hot pudding.

Stravaigin's Award Winning Haggis

by Daniel Blencowe, *Head Chef*, Stravaigin Restaurant

INGREDIENTS

100g suet

1kg mix of lamb's heart, lungs and liver roughly chopped (use only fresh offal)

500ml lamb stock

½ teaspoon ground all spice (or ground pimento berries)

1 teaspoon dried thyme

2 teaspoons cracked black pepper

1 teaspoon salt

400g toasted pinhead oatmeal

1 large Spanish onion roughly chopped

1 large Spanish onion finely chopped

METHOD

Heat the suet in a large saucepan.

Add the roughly chopped onion and offal to the pan and brown.

Remove from the saucepan and mince.

Put the saucepan back on the heat, add the finely chopped onion, fry for a minute then add the minced offal.

Keep stirring and add the pimento berries, thyme and seasoning followed by 400ml lamb stock.

Bring to the boil then reduce the heat and simmer for 3 hours. Stir occasionally and top up with the remaining lamb stock if necessary (should be very moist at this stage).

Add the pinhead oatmeal and cook for a further 10 minutes (or until the oatmeal is al dente), stirring continuously.

The mix should have thickened considerably but add any remaining lamb stock if too dry.

Remove from the heat and serve with mashed neeps, tatties and a final sprinkling of oatmeal for garnish. Don't forget a wee dram of Highland whisky and enjoy.

Stravaigin Restaurant, 28 Gibson Street, Glasgow, G12 8NX
Tel: 0141 334 2665 Fax: 0141 334 4099
Email: stravaigin@btinternet.com www.stravaigin.com

Parsley and Leek Soup

by Steven Doherty, *Managing Director*, Braehead Cook School

INGREDIENTS

Serves: 6

2 small leeks, washed and sliced

2 small onions, peeled and sliced

1 potato, peeled and cut into 6 pieces

2 litres milk

½ litre water

2 cloves of garlic, chopped

1 bunch parsley, picked and washed

Pinch nutmeg

Salt and ground white pepper

METHOD

Method

Put all the prepared vegetables into a large pan and add all the liquids.

Bring to a simmer and cook for 30 minutes.

Taste for seasoning and blend until smooth.

To serve

With fresh bread or oatcakes.

NB

This soup makes a great base or sauce for fish – haddock, cod, salmon, plaice, whiting, smoked haddock and even prawns and langoustines.

Simply garnish the 'soup' base with some fresh cooked vegetables – green beans, broccoli florets, peas, courgettes, sliced cooked new potatoes – then place the fish on top. Make it even healthier by steaming the fish.

Braehead Foods Cook School, 7 Moorfields North Industrial Park, Crosshouse, Kilmarnock, KA2 0FE
Tel: 01563 550008 Fax: 01563 550038
Email: aileen.sales@braeheadfoods.co.uk www.braeheadfoods.co.uk

Supporters

Smoked Mackerel and Creamed Cheese Pâté

by Julie Ireland, *Doctor*, Giffnock, Glasgow

INGREDIENTS

100g butter

150g full fat soft cheese

350g smoked mackerel fillets, skinned and flaked

2 teaspoons lemon juice

1 tablespoon chopped chives

black pepper

4 small bay leaves to garnish (optional)

METHOD

Cream together cheese and 75g of the butter.

Stir in the fish, lemon juice, chives and pepper. Beat mixture until smooth.

Divide mixture between 4 ramekin dishes and smooth the tops.

Melt the rest of the butter in a pan and pour over the dishes. Tip so that the butter forms a thin even film.

Garnish each with a bay leaf if desired.

Can store in fridge for 2 days.

Smoked Scottish Salmon and Cream Cheese Parcels

by Kenny Munro, *Product Manager*, Clarkston, Glasgow

INGREDIENTS

100g fine asparagus

200g tub full fat soft cheese

20g bunch fresh chives, finely chopped, reserving 12 whole chives for garnish

Grated zest of 1 lime

Salt and freshly ground black pepper

200g smoked salmon

METHOD

Blanch the asparagus in a pan of boiling water for 1 minute.

Drain and refresh in cold water.

Remove 5cm from the bottom end of each asparagus spear and finely chop, reserving the tops.

Place the soft cheese, chopped asparagus, chopped chives, lime zest and seasoning in a bowl and mix together well.

Cut the smoked salmon slices into 12 lengths.

Place a spoonful of the soft cheese mixture at one end of each length, top with an asparagus spear and roll up to enclose the filling.

Tie a reserved chive around each parcel.

Oaky Smoked Salmon Stack Potato Cakes

by Angela Murray, *Community Pharmacy Manager*, Stornoway, Isle of Lewis

INGREDIENTS

Salar Flaky Smoked Salmon

Potato Cakes:

250g New Potatoes

250g Butter

1 Egg white

Salt

Coarse Ground Black Pepper

Crème Fraîche Filling

1 large tub of Crème Fraîche

Bunch of spring onions

Several sprigs of chives

Salt

Cayenne pepper

METHOD

Set oven to 180°C.

Wash and peel the potatoes, boil, drain and then mash. Add the butter and lightly whisked egg white and beat to a smooth, creamy mash. Season with salt and a good dash of coarse ground black pepper. Leave to stand for 20 minutes.

Using a dessert spoon, place level spoonfuls of the potato mix onto non-stick baking tray, placing them well apart. Spread and flatten each spoonful into an even, thin disc shape. Place into the oven and bake for 10 minutes or until crisp and golden. Remove from oven and leave to stand for 30 minutes.

Crème Fraîche Filling

Add one tub of crème fraîche into a bowl and season well with salt and cayenne pepper. Finely chop chives and blend into filling mix. Wash and prepare spring onions and chop each onion lengthways, chopping finely into long sprigs.

Final Preparation

Layer flakes of Salar Flaky Smoked Salmon onto the potato cakes and top with crème fraîche filling and garnish with sprigs of spring onion placed on top.

Serve with Rocket and cherry tomatoes, drizzled with olive oil.

A simple yet fantastic starter to any meal.

Superb Thai Soup with Peanut and Chilli Beef

by Anne Roberts, *IS Analyst*, Irvine, Ayrshire

INGREDIENTS

Serves: 4

1 Tin Coconut Milk
4 Tablespoons Olive Oil
1 Tin Water
10g Sea Greens
1 Birds Eye Chilli - sliced
2 Teaspoons Thai Fish Sauce
100g Mixed Mushrooms - sliced
8 Spring Onions - chopped
300g Thick Udon Noodles
50g Spinach – broken into leaves
1 Stock Chicken Cube
2 Garlic Cloves – crushed
Juice of 1 Lime
Zest of 1 Lime – finely grated
Half an onion – chopped
200g Raw Tiger Prawns
100g Thinly Sliced Beef
Sliced Chilli or teaspoon Chilli Oil
1 Tablespoon Peanut Butter
2 Tablespoons Fresh Coriander - chopped

METHOD

Heat half the oil in the pan and add the following and cook for 2 minutes:

Sliced Mushrooms
Chopped Chilli
Chopped Onion

Now add the Coconut Milk, the Water and the Chicken Stock Cube.

Bring to the boil and simmer for 5 minutes.

Now add the following:

Spinach leaves
Chopped Spring Onions
Sea Greens
Fish Sauce
Crushed Garlic
Lime juice and finely grated zest
Chopped Coriander – Keep some back for garnish
Tiger Prawns

Bring back to the boil for 2 minutes.

Now in a separate pan heat the remaining oil.

Toss the Beef in the Peanut Butter and add to the hot oil.

Add the Chilli or Chilli Oil.

Stir Fry until meat is cooked.

To Serve

Heat your plates and put the noodles in the bottom.

Pour the soup over the noodles.

Garnish with the Beef strips and the remaining Coriander leaves.

Carrot, Coconut and Peanut Soup

by Elizabeth Mackinnon, *Solicitor*, Aberdeen

INGREDIENTS

2 tablespoons flora cooking oil

1 potato, grated

6lbs carrots, grated

1 large onion, finely chopped

6 tablespoons coconut cream

2 heaped tablespoons smooth peanut butter

Rounded teaspoon ground ginger

Salt and freshly ground black pepper to season

Swirl of coconut cream sprinkled with chopped chives to garnish

METHOD

Sauté onion in oil and add carrot and potato.

Cover with water, bring to boil and simmer for approx. 30 minutes.

Add coconut cream, peanut butter, ginger and seasoning and simmer for a further 5 minutes.

Remove from heat and liquidise.

Garnish and serve.

Thai Sweet Potato Soup

by Liz Grant, *Physiotherapist*, Newton Mearns, Glasgow

INGREDIENTS

Serves: 3-4

2 Large Sweet Potatoes
1 Onion
Half Teaspoon of Fresh Ginger
2 Garlic Cloves
Half Can Coconut Milk
1 Teaspoon Curry Paste
1 Pint of Chicken Stock
1 Birds Eye Chilli
Chopped Coriander to Garnish

METHOD

Sauté potatoes and onion until onion softens.

Add crushed garlic and ginger.

Pour in coconut milk and chicken stock.

Finally add curry paste and birds eye chilli.

Simmer for 45 mins.

Remove chilli.

Liquidise and serve with chopped coriander.

Chicken & Vegetable Soup

by Doreen Burrows, *Sales Assistant*, Elgin, Morayshire

INGREDIENTS

Serves: 4

Prep time: 1hr 30mins

2 Large Chicken Legs

5 Large Potatoes

1 Medium Turnip

1 Medium Parsnip

3 Medium Carrots

5 Shallots or 2 medium onions

METHOD

Bring to boil 1.5 litres of cold water in a soup pan. While the water is coming up to the boil, wash chicken legs and trim excess fat off them.

Remove outer skins of shallots and roughly chop.

Once water is boiling, add chicken, shallots and seasoning. Reduce the heat to the pan and simmer for 30 minutes.

Whilst making your chicken stock, prepare your remaining ingredients. Peel & dice into 1inch cubes all your vegetables and put to one side ready to add to stock.

After 30 mins remove chicken legs from stock and put aside. Add all your vegetables to the stock and simmer for 45 minutes.

After 45 minutes the vegetables can be blended into the stock using a hand blender. This stage is optional as vegetables can be left whole.

Remove meat from chicken legs and cut into medium pieces. Add to soup and continue to cook for 15 minutes.

Serve soup with fresh bread.

Mixed Nut and Rice Salad

by Audrey Tolland, *Radiography Assistant*, Giffnock, Glasgow

INGREDIENTS

Serves: 4

30mls (2 tbsp) lemon juice

30mls (2 tbsp) olive oil

salt and freshly ground pepper to taste

100g cooked red kidney beans

75g chopped blanched almonds

50g walnuts chopped

50g cashew nuts

150g sultanas

425g can peach slices, drained and chopped

1/4 cucumber, chopped

15mls (1 tbsp) chopped olives

275g cooked long grain rice

METHOD

Mix the olive oil, lemon juice and salt and pepper in a screw top jar and shake vigorously. Soak sultanas in boiling water for 10 mins.

Drain well. Mix the rice, nuts and sultanas. Add the chopped peaches, cucumber, kidney beans and olives. Pour the dressing over the salad and toss lightly.

Serve on a bed of chopped lettuce.

Warm Chicken Salad

by Laura Amner, *Primary School Teacher*, Giffnock, Glasgow

INGREDIENTS

Serves: 4

4 skinless chicken breasts

1 small red pepper (seeded and diced)

1 clove of garlic (crushed)

Freshly ground black pepper

5 tablespoons of extra virgin olive oil

2 tablespoons of clear honey

2 tablespoons of freshly chopped coriander

1 tablespoon of freshly chopped parsley

2 tablespoons of freshly torn basil

Juice of 1 lime

METHOD

Wash the chicken breasts and then dry thoroughly by patting them dry with kitchen towel. Make several slits across the chicken breasts with a sharp knife and place in a non-metallic dish.

Mix all the remaining ingredients together and pour over chicken. Toss the chicken in the mixture to coat them thoroughly. Cover and chill for at least 2 hours, turning halfway.

Preheat oven to fan 190°C/375°F/gas 5. Transfer the chicken to an ovenproof dish and cook for 25-35 minutes, basting once during cooking. Serve with baby potatoes, mixed salad, ciabatta bread and slices of lime.

For an intense flavour, cover and chill the chicken in the marinade for up to 8 hours, or blend the herbs, garlic and oil in a food processor and then cover chicken along with the chopped red pepper. The meat will soak up the strong flavours.

Ready in 2 hours 30 minutes.

Yorkshire Pudding

by Dean Widd, *Regional Advocate Scotland for Action Duchenne*, Stirling

INGREDIENTS

Plain flour

Eggs

Milk

Oil

Dried parsley if desired

METHOD

Using a baking tray designed for Yorkshire puddings, place a half teaspoon of oil in each holder, ensuring the edges have a light coating.

Place the tray in the top part of the oven with the temperature set to 200°C.

While the oil is heating up in the oven we can now look at making the mixture for the puddings.

In a jug/bowl place 2 eggs and beat together.

Now add plain flour to the eggs. To ensure the right mix and amount of flour, combine the flour in the jug with milk and repeat until the mixture is of medium thickness.

Depending on the numberw of puddings you wish to make will determine the amount of mixture required.

If desired add a small amount of dried parsley into the mix to add some colour.

Once the oil is piping hot in the tray carefully empty the mixture into the pudding holders.

Now place the tray back into the oven and increase the heat to 220°C.

Your Yorkshire puddings should be cooked and ready with a light tan colour around the 12 – 15 minute mark.

Enjoy!

Scallop and Pancetta Linguine

by Julie Munro, *Mother to Gregor and Ross*, Clarkston, Glasgow

INGREDIENTS

375g linguine pasta

200g chopped pancetta or bacon lardons (use less if preferred)

200g scallops (fresh or frozen)

2 tablespoons crème fraîche

4 tablespoons freshly grated Parmesan

Olive oil

Handful chopped fresh parsley (optional)

METHOD

Cook the linguine in a large pan of boiling water with a little olive oil until 'al dente'.

Meanwhile, in a large frying pan, cook the bacon or pancetta until crispy (about 5 minutes).

Add the scallops to the pan and fry for a further 5 minutes until the scallops are golden brown and cooked through.

Add the crème fraîche, chopped parsley (if using) and grated parmesan and combine altogether.

Fold the sauce through the cooked pasta and serve immediately.

Tagliatelle with Chicken

by Emma Stirling, *Mum to Ben and Lucy*, Yarrow Valley near Selkirk, Scottish Borders

INGREDIENTS

8oz tagliatelle (fresh or dried)

A jar or sachet of tomato and basil pasta sauce (you can make your own)

2oz of butter

14oz of chicken breast cut into strips

3oz of blanched almonds (found in the cooking aisle)

Half a pint of double cream

Salt and pepper

Tomato and basil sauce

1 Small onion, chopped

1 garlic clove, crushed

1 tbsp olive oil

200g / 7 oz can chopped tomatoes

2 tsp tomato puree (paste)

½ tsp sugar

½ tsp dried oregano

1 bay leaf

salt and pepper

METHOD

To make chicken part of the dish, melt the butter in the pan and fry the chicken strips and the almonds for about 5 mins or until chicken is cooked.

Meanwhile, heat up the cream in a small pan, bring to the boil and boil for about 10 mins (over a low heat). Once the cream has reduced by half, pour over the chicken and almonds, stir well and set aside in a warm place.

Cook your pasta according to instruction and heat up the pasta sauce. Then once everything is cooked assemble the dish. First the pasta then the pasta sauce and finish with the chicken and almond mixture and serve.

For the tomato and basil sauce

Fry the onion and garlic gently in the oil for 5 minutes until softened but not browned.

Add the tomatoes, tomato purée (paste), sugar, oregano, bay leaf and seasoning. Stir well.

Bring to the boil, then cover and simmer gently for 20 minutes, stirring occasionally, until you have a thickish sauce.

Remove the bay leaf and adjust seasoning to taste. This sauce keeps well in a screw-top jar in the fridge for up to a week.

You can add a chopped fresh chilli when frying the onions for a spicy sauce.

Lasagne

by Mairi Maclugash, *Accountant*, Isle of Islay

INGREDIENTS

Meat Sauce

2 tbsp olive oil

1kg or 2lb minced beef

4/5 slices of smoked bacon, chopped

45g or 1½ oz plain flour

300ml or ½ pint of beef stock

2 x 400g or 13oz cans of chopped tomatoes

2 onions, finely chopped

2 large cloves of garlic, crushed

8 tbsp tomato puree

Salt & black pepper to taste

Mushrooms (optional)

White Sauce

90g or 3 oz butter

70g or 2½ oz flour

900ml or 1½ pints of milk

200g or 7oz of grated mature cheddar

45g or 1½ oz grated parmesan

Easy cook dry lasagne sheets

METHOD

Heat the oil in a large pan and brown beef. Add the onions and bacon and cook for a further five minutes. Stir in the flour and add stock, tomatoes, onions, garlic, tomato puree and season to taste. Add some chopped mushrooms at this stage if desired. Bring to the boil, cover and simmer gently for 1 hour.

To make white sauce, melt the butter in a saucepan, stir in the flour and blend for 1 minute, stirring all the time. Gradually add the milk, stirring continuously to prevent lumps from forming. Bring to the boil to thicken. Add approx. two thirds of the cheese to the sauce and allow to melt, then season with salt and pepper.

Spoon a third of the meat sauce into a lasagne dish and cover with a layer of lasagne sheets. Pour over a third of the white sauce. Continue building two further layers of each, finishing with a layer of white sauce which should be topped with the remaining cheese.

Bake in a preheated oven at 190°C (375°F, gas mark five) for 45-55 minutes until the pasta is cooked and the top golden and bubbling.

Enjoy!

Haggis Lasagne

by Alberto Marioni (age 95), *Former Owner of the Central Café*, Fraserburgh, Aberdeenshire

INGREDIENTS

1 haggis
Dozen sheets of lasagne
Dozen cherry tomatoes
Salt and freshly ground pepper

For the sauce

3oz butter
3oz plain flour
1 pint milk
4oz freshly grated Parmesan cheese

METHOD

Preheat oven to 180°C/350°F/Gas Mark 4.

Cut open the haggis and crumble most of it over the base of a greased lasagne dish.

Place lasagne sheets on top and then add the remaining haggis.

To make the sauce, melt the butter and stir in the flour to form a roux.

Gradually add the milk, continually stirring to avoid lumps forming.

Stir for 5 minutes then season to taste.

Add tomatoes to half of the sauce and pour over the layer of haggis.

Top with lasagne and finish with a layer of the remaining white sauce and cheese sprinkled on top.

Bake in oven for approx. 45 minutes or until the pasta is cooked.

Serve with a leafy salad.

Savoury Macaroni Cheese

by Susan Anderson, *Bank Manager*, Grangemouth, Stirlingshire

INGREDIENTS

250g/9oz macaroni

40g/1½oz butter

40g/1½ plain flour

600ml/1pint 1½fl oz milk

250g/9oz grated cheddar

Packet good quality pork sausages, grilled & chopped into bite sizes pieces.

450g/16oz tin chopped tomatoes

METHOD

Cook the pasta in a large saucepan of boiling salted water according to packet instructions; drain well and set aside.

Melt the butter over a medium heat in a saucepan slightly larger than that used for the pasta. Add the flour and stir to form a roux, cooking for a few minutes.

Gradually whisk in the milk, a little at a time. Cook for 5 minutes to a thickened and smooth sauce.

Meanwhile, preheat the grill to hot.

Remove the sauce from the hob, add 175g/6oz of the cheese and stir until the cheese is well combined and melted.

Add the macaroni to the sauce and mix well. Stir through the cooked sausages & tomatoes. Transfer to a deep, suitably-sized ovenproof dish.

Sprinkle over the remaining cheddar and cook for 15 / 20 mins at 200°C / Gas mark 6.

The cheese should be browned and bubbling. Serve straightaway.

This is a recipe that I was taught 30 years ago in my domestic science class, it is really easy to make. I still cook it regularly because my domestic science skills have not improved over the years.

Chicken & Asparagus Risotto

by William Mackay, *Modern Studies Teacher*, Barrhead, Glasgow

INGREDIENTS

3-4 Chicken Supremes - Diced

1 Bunch of fresh asparagus - cut to 1inch long

250 grams of Arborio rice

Chicken stock (approx. litre)

2 strands of saffron (or sprinkle of powdered type)

Cracked black pepper

Parmesan cheese shavings

METHOD

Dice the chicken supremes and place in a large heated sauté pan with a teaspoon of olive oil.

Keep turning until chicken turns white. Add asparagus to pan and stir through chicken for 2-3 minutes.

Add rice to pan and mix with chicken and asparagus.

Allow to cook for 1-2 minutes, stirring continuously. Add sprinkle of pepper.

Cover the mixture fully with chicken stock.

Add saffron strands/powder. Stir often. Mix will be cooked in 7-8 minutes, as stock is reduced by rice expanding.

Fold parmesan shavings through mixture before serving.

Oven Baked Chicken

by Anne Duncan, *Teacher (retired)*, Aberdeen

INGREDIENTS

4 chicken portions

2 oz butter

2½ oz plain crisps

4 oz white grated cheese

1 tablespoon parsley (optional)

½ teaspoon garlic powder (optional)

½ teaspoon dried tarragon

Salt and pepper

METHOD

Melt butter and brush half over chicken.

Crush crisps and mix with remaining ingredients. Season to taste.

Press mixture around chicken portions and place on a baking tray or ovenproof dish.

Pour over the remaining butter.

Bake in preheated oven (180°C/350°F/Gas 4) for 45 minutes (or until the chicken is tender and juices run clear).

Serve with baked potato and sweetcorn or a side salad and crusty bread.

Chicken Enchiladas

by Julie Mitchell-Mehta, *Marketing Consultant*, Aboyne, Aberdeenshire

INGREDIENTS

4 chicken breasts

2 green chillies – sliced and seeds removed

4 tbsp lime juice

2 tbsp vegetable oil

1 red pepper - sliced

1 green pepper - sliced

1 medium onion - sliced

2 cloves garlic – finely chopped

200 ml crème fraîche

1 tin chopped tomatoes

3 tbsp salsa

Grated cheddar

8 flour tortillas

METHOD

Chop the chicken breasts into strips and marinate in a large bowl with the lime juice and the chopped chillies for at least 1 hour.

Preheat the oven to 180°C.

In a large frying pan, heat the oil and fry the onions until softened. Add the sliced peppers, garlic and the chicken with its marinade and cook on a high heat for 10 – 15 minutes until the chicken is cooked through and golden.

Grease a large ovenproof dish. Take a tortilla, spread with crème fraîche and place a large spoonful of the chicken and vegetable mixture in a line along the centre. Roll up the tortilla and place, with the join downwards, in the dish. Repeat with the rest of the tortillas.

In a bowl, mix the chopped tomatoes and the salsa and spread evenly over the top of the tortillas. Top with the grated cheese and cook in the oven for 30 minutes.

Chicken Tagine

by Audrey Rosenbaum & Valerie Dowie, *The Duloch Discovery*, Dalgety Bay, Fife

INGREDIENTS

Serves: 6

2 tbsp olive oil

4 chicken breasts, halved

1 onion, chopped

2 tsp grated fresh root ginger

Pinch saffron or turmeric

Pinch cinnamon (optional)

Pinch cumin (optional)

1 tbsp honey

400g carrots cut into sticks

Small bunch roughly chopped parsley

Lemon wedges to serve

METHOD

Heat the oil in a large, wide pan with a lid. Add the chicken and fry quickly until light coloured. Add the onion and ginger then fry for a further 2 minutes.

Add 150ml water, the saffron, cinnamon, cumin, honey and carrots; season, then stir well. Bring to the boil, cover tightly and simmer for 15 minutes or until the chicken is tender.

Uncover and increase the heat for about 5 minutes to reduce the sauce a little.

Sprinkle with parsley and serve with lemon wedges for squeezing over.

Chicken Thighs with Lime, Honey and Chilli

by Joan Omand, *Pupil Support Assistant*, Deaconsbank, Glasgow

INGREDIENTS

4-6 chicken thighs (on the bone with skin on)

Zest and juice of 2 limes

4 tablespoons clear honey

1 fat garlic clove, peeled and crushed

½ tsp crushed dried chillies

Salt

METHOD

Preheat oven 220°C.

Put thighs in single layer on roasting tin or ovenproof dish.

In a bowl, mix lime zest and juice, honey, garlic and chillies and season with salt.

Pour the mixture over the chicken and coat.

Roast for 1 hour or until chicken well cooked, basting 2 or 3 times until sticky and golden.

Serve with your choice of vegetables.

Chicken and Chestnut

by Aileen Johnston, *Surveyor*, Glasgow

INGREDIENTS

(Amounts are not critical, vary according to taste and how much chicken you've got left)

Leftover roast chicken, chopped

2 sticks of celery, chopped

1 can of water chestnuts (220g), chopped

1 can of condensed chicken soup

Generous tablespoon of mayonnaise.

1 small packet of plain crisps

METHOD

Mix everything together, except the crisps, and put into an oven proof baking dish. Bake in the oven for about 20 minutes at 190°C.

Crush the packet of crisps and sprinkle over the top. Put under the grill until browned.

Serve with boiled rice.

Mango Chicken

by June Reid, *Accounts Assistant,* Clarkston, Glasgow

INGREDIENTS

4 chopped chicken breasts

3 dessertspoons lemon or lime juice

2 dessertspoons Worcestershire sauce

4 dessertspoons mayonnaise

4 dessertspoons mango chutney

1 courgette, chopped (optional)

8 small mushrooms, chopped (optional)

METHOD

Mix the chicken and lemon or lime juice in an ovenproof dish.

Add the Worcestershire sauce, mayonnaise and mango chutney and stir.

Mix in the courgette and mushrooms or your own choice of vegetables.

Cover and cook at 200°C for 40-45 mins.

Serve with rice or potatoes.

Chicken Bhuna Curry

by Neil Morrison, *Expatriate Scot*, San Diego, California, USA

INGREDIENTS

Cooking time: 20 minutes

Serves: 3-4

2 medium boneless skinless chicken breasts, cut into 2cm cubes

5 tablespoons of vegetable oil

1 medium onion, cut in half, chop one half finely, grate the other half roughly

2 cloves garlic - grated roughly and chopped

1 green chilli pepper finely chopped (optional – leave out for kids recipe)

Sprinkle of Salt and Season all to taste

Half a teaspoon of mild curry paste (Patak's) or half a teaspoon of mild curry powder

2 fresh ripe tomatoes, chopped

Cup of Basmati rice

2 cups of water

Pinch of salt

3 teaspoons of vegetable oil

METHOD

Into medium saucepan add the oil and heat on medium heat.

Add the chopped onions and stir until they start to turn golden brown.

Add the chopped garlic and the optional green chilli pepper, stir for 2 minutes.

Add the chicken breasts, stir for 3 minutes until the chicken turns white.

Add a good sprinkle of salt and seasoning to taste.

Add the curry paste still under medium heat and stir.

Add the grated onion and heat for 4 minutes.

Add the chopped tomatoes under a medium heat and stir gently until a smooth sauce forms.

Reduce heat to low and heat for a further 5 minutes to reduce and serve.

To another saucepan with lid add the oil and salt under very low heat.

Add the cup of Basmati rice to the pan and stir until the oil coats the rice.

Add two cups of newly boiled water.

Bring to boil, cover pan with lid and leave on lowest heat for 12 minutes.

Turn off heat, stir and cover and leave for a further 10 minutes.

Guff's Homemade Chicken Curry

by Iain Macdonald, *Consultant Design Engineer*, Polmont, Falkirk

INGREDIENTS

8 Small Chicken Pieces
1 Large Tin of Tomatoes
4 Large Onions
2/3 Heaped tsp Hot Curry Powder
1 tsp Cumin
1 tsp Ground Cloves
1 tsp Ginger, Cinnamon
1 tsp Coriander
1 tsp Cardamon
1 tsp Tumeric
1 tsp Black Pepper
1 tsp Salt
1 tsp Garlic Powder
1 tsp Chilli Powder
2 tsp Garam Masala
1 tsp Paprika.

METHOD

Purify the Onions and Tomatoes using a blender. Melt a knob of butter in a large pan.

Add the purified Onions and Tomatoes and spices. Cook on high for about 3 minutes until the mixture has blended together. Lastly add the Chicken Pieces and stir to coat.

Cover and simmer for about an hour and a half until the meat is tender.

Helpful hint:

It is best to lay out all the spices on a plate first so they can be added all at one time.

Additional Chicken Stock can be added if the mixture is too dense.

Sweet Turkey Curry

by Helen Lyburn, *Housewife*, Prestwick, Ayrshire

INGREDIENTS

1lb chopped cooked turkey

2 small jars of cranberry sauce

1 large chopped onion

1 tablespoon plain flour

2oz butter

2 tablespoons tomato paste

2 tablespoons mild curry powder

1 clove of garlic

3 bay leaves

3 cloves

Salt to taste

1 pint of water

METHOD

Melt butter in pan, add chopped onion and garlic and cook for 2 minutes.

Remove from heat and add cranberry sauce, tomato paste, curry powder, flour and salt and mix together.

Gradually add water, keep stirring and return to heat.

Bring to the boil and add cloves and bay leaves.

Reduce heat and simmer for 30 minutes until mixture thickens.

Remove bay leaves and cloves .

Add turkey and stir through sauce.

Serve with rice.

Turkey Milano

by Marie Buchan, *Teacher (Retired)*, Aberdeen

INGREDIENTS

3ozs butter

1 small green pepper, finely sliced

4 large mushrooms, sliced

2ozs plain flour

¾ pint chicken stock

300ml carton soured cream

12ozs spaghetti

2 large tomatoes, chopped

1 clove garlic

12ozs cooked turkey

2 egg yolks

Small carton double cream

2ozs grated Parmesan cheese for topping

Seasoning, if required

METHOD

Fry pepper and mushroom slices in butter.

Add flour and stock to make a smooth sauce.

Cook for 3 minutes then stir in soured cream, tomatoes, garlic and cooked turkey.

Do not allow to boil.

Finally mix in egg yolks and double cream.

Leave to cool then pour into casserole and cover with foil.

Meanwhile, cook spaghetti 'al dente'.

Drain and mix well into turkey mixture in casserole.

Sprinkle with grated Parmesan cheese.

Put in moderate oven and cook for 30 minutes or until browned on top.

Serve with green salad.

Duck with Star Anise

by Julie Duncanson, *Actress*, Milngavie, Glasgow

INGREDIENTS

Serves: 3-4

8 large duck pieces (legs, breast etc) on the bone

2 tbsp ground nut oil

2 onions

6 (yes 6) large and juicy cloves of garlic

8 'coins' of fresh ginger

8 spring onions

2 tsp of palm (or ordinary) sugar

500ml chicken stock

125ml rice wine (dry sherry if desperate)

3 whole star anise

METHOD

Set oven to 180°C gas mark 4.

Warm oil in heavy casserole dish then lightly brown the duck pieces. Peel and roughly chop the onions. Lift the duck onto a plate.

Add onions; turn down heat and let cook, giving the occasional stir until soft and sweet.

Peel garlic, slice each clove thinly and stir into onions. Cut ginger into matchsticks and add. Cut spring onions in short lengths and add and stir until softened. Stir in palm sugar, chicken stock, wine and star anise. Season with black pepper and salt and bring to boil.

Let cool for a good minute then return meat and any juices that have been released. Cover with lid, transfer to oven and set timer for 1hour and 15mins. When time is up, check duck for tenderness. It should be soft but far from falling off the bone.

Season with salt then lift duck onto plates and spoon over sauce.

Serve with rice.

I once made this for the wonderful Mr Ian Heggie, one of Scotland's finest living playwrights when he came round to dinner just after my beautiful son Joel was born. He loved it, so do I and I hope you do too.

Stuffed Fillet of Pork

by Carolyn Richards, *Solicitor*, Aberdeen

INGREDIENTS

5oog (1 lb) piece of lean pork fillet

Small bunch of basil leaves (washed)

2 tbsp grated Parmesan

2 tbsp sun-dried tomato paste

6 thin slices of streaky bacon or Parma ham

1 tbsp olive oil

Salt & pepper

METHOD

Trim away the excess fat and membrane from the pork fillet. Slice the pork lengthways down the middle, taking care not to cut all the way through.

Open out the pork and season down the inside. Lay the basil leaves down the centre.

Mix the cheese and sun dried tomato paste and spread on top of the basil.

Press the pork back together and wrap the ham around the pork, overlapping to cover.

Place on a rack in a roasting tin, seam-side down and brush with olive oil.

Bake in a hot oven (180°C) for 30-40 minutes depending on thickness until cooked through. Allow to stand for 10 minutes.

Drain the cooked pork and slice thinly to serve either with roast or boiled and crushed potatoes, braised red cabbage and vegetables of your choice or alternatively with a tossed salad and crusty bread.

Meat Loaf

by Margaret McKay, *Housewife*, Alloway, Ayrshire

INGREDIENTS

1lb steak mince

¾lb smoked bacon

2 slices of fresh breadcrumbs

1 egg

1 teaspoon dry mustard

1 teaspoon mixed herbs

Salt and pepper

METHOD

Mix all the ingredients together in a large bowl.

Steam for 2 hours.

Stuffed Peppers

by Liz Kennedy, *Managing Director*, Arkay Sales, Carmunnock, Glasgow

INGREDIENTS

Serves: 6

1 pepper per person

1lb mince

1 onion, chopped

Some crushed chilli flakes or Tabasco (optional)

a few mushrooms, chopped

a few dashes of Lea & Perrins

1 tin chopped tomatoes

pinch dried mixed herbs

1 pkt cooked rice

salt & pepper

METHOD

Cut peppers in half lengthways, leaving the stalks on. This helps keep the shape.

De-seed and place in microwave for about 5 mins to soften.

Soften the onions in some oil and then add the mince and cook until browned.

Add all ingredients except the mushrooms.

Mix and cook for 30 minutes.

Then add the mushrooms and cook for a further 10 mins.

If the mixture gets too dry add some stock or water.

Fill an ovenproof dish with about an inch of water.

Fill the peppers with the mince and place in the dish.

Dot the peppers with butter and bake in the oven at 180°C for 30 mins.

Serve the peppers with cheese sauce.

Enjoy…

Braised Lamb Shank with Mash and Malt Whisky Gravy

by John Saunderson, *Butcher*, Edinburgh

INGREDIENTS

Serves: 2

2 Scotch lamb shanks

1 carrot, peeled & chopped

1 onion, peeled & chopped

1 leek, chopped

2 garlic cloves, peeled & chopped

250ml (½ pint) lamb stock

60ml (4 tbsp) malt whisky

450g (1lb) potatoes, cooked & mashed

Vegetable oil

Salt & pepper

METHOD

Heat oil in a heavy based pan or casserole dish. Season lamb shanks and brown on all sides. Add chopped vegetables, garlic and stock and bring to a simmer. Place in a medium oven 170°C, 325°F, Gas Mark 3 and cook for approx. 2 hours, turning shanks once or twice during cooking. Meat should be just falling off the bone when cooked. Strain cooking juices in to a pan, add the whisky and reduce by one third (to thicken the sauce a little, mash in some of the cooking vegetables) and check seasoning. Place the mashed potato in the centre of a large plate. Put lamb shank on top with shank pointing up and spoon sauce around.

Serve with French beans and puy lentils or seasonal vegetables.

HIGH CLASS
JOHN
SAUNDERSON
FAMILY BUTCHER
1958
Est. 50 Years
2008

40 Leven Street, Edinburgh, EH3 9LJ
Tel: 0131 229 8348
e-mail: shop@johnsaunderson.co.uk www.johnsaunderson.co.uk

Stew

by Annie Munro, *Senior Social Care Worker (retired)*, Stornoway, Isle of Lewis

INGREDIENTS

1 tablespoon olive oil
1 large chopped onion
1 minced garlic clove
Seasoned plain flour
2lbs diced stewing steak
2 tablespoons tomato purée
3-4 sliced carrots
3-4 sliced parsnips
¼ pint red wine
¾ pint beef stock
Salt and freshly ground black pepper

METHOD

Preheat the oven to 150°C/300°F.

Heat the oil in a large flameproof casserole then gently fry onion and garlic until softened.

Coat the stew with seasoned flour and brown in casserole before adding the carrots, parsnips and purée. Pour in stock and red wine, stir then bring to the boil and cover.

Place in the oven for 3-4 hours, stirring once or twice during that time.

Season to taste then serve with mashed potato.

Sausage and Tomato Casserole

by Stella Murphy, *Invoice Administrator*, Strathaven, South Lanarkshire

INGREDIENTS

4 beef sausages
1 sliced onion
1 clove garlic
400g can chopped tomatoes
1 can butter beans, drained
1 chopped carrot
2 teaspoons tomato purée
Pinch dried mixed herbs
Pinch sugar

METHOD

Spray non-stick pan with a little oil.

Fry the sausages, onion and garlic for 4-5 minutes.

Cut the sausages into slices.

Add the remaining ingredients and bring to the boil.

Cover and simmer for 20 minutes.

Serve with mashed potatoes and peas.

Pan Fried Crusted Cod with Quick Curry Sauce

by Belle Mackay, *Primary Teacher*, Laxdale, Isle of Lewis

INGREDIENTS

4 thick, skinless cod fillets

1 red chilli (or two for a spicier sauce)

2 finely chopped shallots

2 peeled and chopped garlic cloves

2 stems lemon grass, white part only, finely chopped

4 fresh coriander roots, chopped

2 teaspoons lime rind

Half a teaspoon drained green peppercorns chopped

125 ml olive oil

125ml coconut milk

1 tablespoon fish sauce

4 kaffir lime leaves, finely chopped

2 tablespoons lime juice

METHOD

Stick the red chilli or chillies in boiling water for 15 minutes, drain and chop finely.

Put the chopped chilli, shallots, garlic, lemongrass, coriander roots, lime rind, peppercorns and a good glug of oil in a food processor and mix into a smooth paste.

Spread the paste on both sides of the fish.

Add the remaining oil to a frying pan and cook the fish for about 3 minutes, both sides.

In another pan add the kaffir leaves, coconut milk, lime juice and simmer for about 3 minutes.

After removing the kaffir leaves, add to the pan with the fish and simmer for about 2/3 minutes. Best with Muscadet or even fantastic NZ wine like "Mount Difficulty".

A Meaty Fish Dish

by Charlie Afrin, *Head Chef*, Merchiston Castle School, Edinburgh

INGREDIENTS

Serves: 4

Monkfish Tail (off the bone), 5-6 oz

One Slice of Parma Ham

3 oz Chorizo Sausage

1 Slice Stornoway Black Pudding

Crushed New Potatoes

Olive Oil

METHOD

Preheat the oven to 220°C, Gas Mark 7.

Wrap the Monkfish Tail with the Parma Ham.

Place it on a non stick baking tray with one slice of Stornoway Black Pudding and put it into the preheated oven for approx. 8-10 mins depending on the thickness of the Monkfish. The Monkfish should be firm to the touch when cooked.

Cut the Chorizo in to half inch pieces and pan fry in a little olive oil until the oil in the pan turns red.

Put the Crushed New Potatoes in the centre of the plate with the Stornoway Black pudding on top. Slice the Monkfish at an angle and place on top.

Place the Chorizo around the Monkfish and drizzle the oil around the outside of the dish.

Serve with wilted Spinach or Purple Sprouting Broccoli.

Prawns and Noodles in Coconut Milk

by Pauline Maclean, *Solicitor*, Blanefield, Glasgow

INGREDIENTS

Meat Sauce

400g cooked prawns

2 tablespoons walnut oil

3 shallots, peeled and finely chopped

2 garlic cloves, peeled and finely chopped

½ teaspoon ground turmeric

1 teaspoon ground coriander

2 pinches chilli powder

Pinch ground cardamom

Piece root ginger, grated

2 individual sachets creamed coconut

Thin egg noodles

Chopped fresh parsley or coriander

Pint fish stock

METHOD

Heat oil and cook shallots gently until soft, stirring constantly.

Add garlic, turmeric, coriander, chilli powder, cardamom and grated ginger.

Stir well and cook 5 minutes.

Add stock and stir in coconut.

Bring to boil and bubble until coconut melted.

Simmer until reduced by half.

Add noodles and prawns and cook until noodles tender.

Sprinkle with a little salt, lots of chopped parsley or coriander and serve immediately.

Grilled Langoustines with a Pernod and Olive Oil Dressing

by Ali Matheson, *North Sea Welder*, Balloch, Inverness-shire

INGREDIENTS

Serves: 4

16 large langoustines
2 small shallots, finely chopped
1/2 tablespoon roughly chopped tarragon
1/2 tablespoon roughly chopped flat-leaf parsley
1 teaspoon dijon mustard
1 teaspoon dark soy sauce
85ml(3fl oz) extra virgin olive oil
1 1/2 tablespoons fresh lemon juice
1 teaspoon Pernod
50 g (2oz) butter melted
salt and freshly ground pepper.

METHOD

Pre-heat the grill to high.

Cut the langoustines open lengthways and scoop out the creamy contents of the heads and any red row with a tea spoon.

Put this into a small bowl and stir in the shollots, tarragon, parsley, mustard, soy sauce, oil, lemon juice, Pernod and a little salt and pepper to taste.

Place the half langoustines cut side up on a baking tray or the rack of the grill pan and brush with the melted butter.

Season lightly and grill for 2 or 3 minutes until the shells and the meat are heated through.

Put the langoustines on 4 serving plates and spoon over a little of the dressing.

Divide the rest of the dressing between 4 dipping saucers or ramekins and serve.

Tuna Steaks in a Chinese Marinade

by Elaine Jamieson, *Primary School Teacher*, Aberdeen

INGREDIENTS

4 Tuna Steaks
1 tablespoon Brown Sugar
1 Tablespoon Sesame oil
100ml Soy Sauce
100ml Rice Wine Vinegar
2 garlic cloves (crushed)
¼ inch of Fresh Grated Garlic
Black pepper
2 Teaspoons Dried Chilli Flakes

METHOD

Mix all the marinade ingredients together in a jug.

Pour the marinade into a Ziploc bag.

Place the Tuna Steaks in the bag and seal.

Put the bag in the fridge and leave for at least four hours, ideally leave to marinate overnight.

Spray a griddle pan with oil and put it on the heat.

When the pan is very hot cook the tuna for 2-3 minutes on each side (depending on the thickness of the steaks and how you prefer it cooked).

Serve with salad and Rice.

An Aussie Sponge Cake

by The McKnights, *Expatriate Scots*, Sydney, Australia

INGREDIENTS

4 free range eggs (at room temperature)

2/3 cup caster sugar

1/3 cup corn flour

1/3 cup plain flour

1/3 cup self-raising flour

Topping:

250ml double cream

3 tablespoons icing sugar

½ punnet strawberries or shaved dark chocolate

Raspberry jam

METHOD

Beat the eggs until light and creamy. This usually takes about 7 minutes with an electric hand mixer. Gradually add the caster sugar, beating well after each addition.

Sift the corn flour, plain flour and self-raising flour together. Lightly fold this through the mixture.

Spoon the mixture into 2 greased 20cm deep cake tins.

Bake at 180°C for 20 minutes or until golden. Turn onto a wire rack to cool.

Whip the cream and icing sugar until thick. Spread a generous layer of raspberry jam on one of the sponges and then top with half the whipped cream. Sandwich the sponges together. Top with the remaining cream and decorate with sliced strawberries or shaved dark chocolate.

Christmas Cake

by Katherine Urquhart, *B&B Owner*, Bridgend, Isle of Islay

INGREDIENTS

4oz glacé cherries

8oz each currants, sultanas, seedless raisins

2oz mixed peel

4floz brandy or whisky

8oz butter

8oz soft brown sugar

4 eggs

8oz plain flour

1tsp mixed spice

1tsp cinnamon

½ tsp ginger

½ nutmeg

2 tbsp milk

Sornbank B&B, Bridgend, Isle of Islay, http://www.sornbank.co.uk/

METHOD

Grease 8in round deep cake tin. Cut two circles of greaseproof paper to fit base of tin. Line rest of cake tin with greaseproof.

Rinse cherries, drain well and cut into quarters. Place cherries, dried fruit and mixed peel into bowl, pour over brandy and stir well and leave overnight.

Beat the butter until soft and pale and gradually beat in the sugar until blended. Mix the eggs in a jug and slowly add them to the creamed mixture. After each egg, it should have a smooth consistency.

Sift together flour, mixed spice, cinnamon, ginger and nutmeg. Using a large metal spoon, gently fold in the flour into creamed mixture. Don't beat or the texture of the cake will change. Add milk and dried fruit and spoon into tin and level surface.

Tie a double band of brown paper around cake tin as this stops the edges from burning.

Bake at 150°C/300°F/mark 2 for about 3 ½ hrs or until skewer comes out clean. If browning too quick cover lightly with tin foil.

Skewer surface of cake and add a little more brandy and leave to soak in.

Turn cake out when cool and wrap in greaseproof and foil.

Store in a cool, dry place for up to 3 months.

Quick and Easy Fruit Loaf

by Beth Millin, *Sales Manager*, Catrine, Ayrshire

INGREDIENTS

Preparation time: **15 minutes**

Cooking time: **1-2 hours**

1 cup raisins

1 cup sultanas

1 cup sugar

1 cup water

125g/4oz margarine

2 cups self raising flour

2 eggs

1 tsp baking soda

METHOD

Put the raisins, sultanas, margarine, water and sugar into a pot and bring to the boil. Simmer and stir for approx. 10 minutes until the fruit is softened. Add the flour, eggs and baking powder. Beat for 1 minute.

Line a loaf tin with baking or greaseproof paper and pour in the mixture.

Put in oven at 180°C and bake for approx. 1 hour 45 minutes to 2 hours depending on type of oven.

Lemon Freeze Recipe

by Sue Cameron-Nebolisa, *Administrator*, Dunning, Perthshire

INGREDIENTS

Serves: 4

3 oz of crushed cornflakes

2 eggs separated

5 tablespoons caster sugar

1 oz melted butter

small can (170g) condensed milk

4-5 tablespoons lemon juice

METHOD

Blend together the cornflake crumbs, melted butter and 2 tablespoons of sugar. Press all but 5 tablespoons into the bottom of a plastic dish (approx. 9.5″ long x 5.5″ wide).

Beat egg yolks in a deep bowl until thick and creamy. Combine with the condensed milk. Add the lemon juice and stir until thickened (2-3 minutes).

Beat egg whites stiff and gradually beat in last 3 tablespoons of sugar, fold through lemon mix then pour into tray and sprinkle on top the remaining 5 tablespoons of crushed cornflakes.

Put in freezer for a minimum of 2 hours then slice and serve.

Clootie Dumpling

by Joan Mackay, *currently Full Time Mother*, Edinburgh

INGREDIENTS

1lb plain flour

8oz suet

8oz sugar (brown is good)

8oz raisins

8oz currants

2 level teaspoons bicarbonate of soda

2 level teaspoons ginger

2 level teaspoons cinnamon

2 level teaspoons mixed spice

2 to 3 level dessertspoons syrup (melted)

2 to 3 level dessertspoons treacle (melted)

2 eggs (beaten)

milk

You will also need

a large pan

a plate that can withstand boiling water (Pyrex is good) with a diameter less than the size of the pan base

a large square piece of cotton (a white pillow case opened up will do the job)

METHOD

Prepare pan of boiling water. Begin with approx. 2 pints of water and top up later as needed.

Mix all dry ingredients together in a large bowl.

Add melted syrup, treacle and beaten eggs and mix to a flexible but stiff consistency. Use milk if needed to achieve this consistency.

Scald the cotton cloth in the boiling water then ring out and dredge with flour.

Spoon dumpling mixture into centre of cloth and tie up with string, leaving space for the dumpling to expand. (A large adult fist size worth of space should do).

Place clootie dumpling on plate in the boiling water.

Keep water boiling briskly throughout the process. Top up water as needed from a boiling kettle and pour water down the side of the pan (not onto dumpling). The water should not come over the top of the dumpling but should sit between half and two thirds of its size.

Allow 3 1/2 to 4 hours cooking time. The dumpling should be ready when it feels firm when pressed with a wooden spoon.

Turn the dumpling out onto a large plate and dry off or keep warm until needed in an oven heated to no more than 100°C.

Clootie dumpling is delicious served on its own or with the following options: fresh cream, custard, vanilla ice cream, crème fraîche.

It is ideal when entertaining a large group of people on a cold day and with mulled wine when in season. It is very popular with most children.

Light Gingerbread

by Alison Sim, Inverness

INGREDIENTS

8oz plain flour

4oz margarine

1 egg

2oz granulated sugar

8oz golden syrup

1 teaspoon mixed spice

1 teaspoon baking soda

2 teaspoon ground ginger

¼ pint milk

METHOD

Put margarine and syrup in pan and heat gently until margarine is melted.

Cool slightly and add to the dry ingredients.

Warm the milk in the same pan, making sure all syrup has been used.

Pour the milk over the ingredients and beat thoroughly.

Beat in the egg and stir then pour into lined loaf tin.

Bake at gas 1-2 (135-150°C) for approximately 1-1¼ hours.

Fresh Lemon Cake

by Doranne Murray, *Health Visitor (Retired)*, Aberdeen

INGREDIENTS

4oz soft margarine
6oz self raising flour
1 level teaspoon baking powder
6oz caster sugar
2 eggs
4 tablespoons milk
Grated rind of 1 lemon

For topping

Juice of 1 lemon
4oz caster sugar

METHOD

Preheat oven 180°C/350°F/gas mark 4.

Grease and line an 8″ round tin with grease proof paper (loose bottom tin helps).

Put all ingredients into a large bowl and mix well for a couple of minutes.

Turn mixture into the tin and bake for approx. 50-60 minutes or when cake has shrunk from the sides of the tin and springs back when pressed in the centre.

Mix the juice of the lemon with the sugar and spread this over the hot cake.

Leave in the tin until cold and then turn out.

It is a good idea to mix the lemon juice and the sugar as soon as you put the cake into the oven and stir it from time to time to dissolve.

To make this cake a special treat, fill the centre, once you split it in two, with a mixture of ½ pint cream whipped loosely and 4 tablespoons of good lemon curd mixed through.

Rice Cake

by Joy Taylor, *Housewife*, Troon, Ayrshire

INGREDIENTS

6ozs caster sugar

6ozs butter (unsalted and at room temperature)

2 eggs

4ozs self raising flour

4ozs ground rice

Few drops almond or vanilla essence

3 tablespoons milk

METHOD

Line a 2lb loaf tin with baking parchment.

Sift together the flour and ground rice.

Cream together the butter and sugar.

Add the beaten eggs one at a time to the creamed mixture.

Gently fold in the flour to the mixture.

Add essence and milk to make a soft consistency.

Transfer to the loaf tin and bake in middle shelf of moderate oven (gas 4 or 130-140°C) for about 1 hour and 10 minutes.

Cool on wire rack (remove parchment after about 20 minutes).

This recipe has been enjoyed by several generations of my family – it came down from my Great Grandmother and is enjoyed today by my grandchildren.

Seven Cup Steamed Dumpling

by Mabel Revel, *Teacher*, Banchory, Kincardineshire

INGREDIENTS

1 cup self-raising flour

1 cup suet

1 cup milk

1 cup currants

1 cup raisins

1 cup breadcrumbs

1 cup sugar

2 level teaspoons ground cinnamon

1 level teaspoon baking soda

1 egg

METHOD

Generously grease a 1.2 litre pudding basin and line the base with a circle of greaseproof paper. Cut out and grease a 25cm square of foil.

Whisk together milk and egg.

Mix together all ingredients in mixing bowl and transfer mixture to pudding basin.

Place the foil on a work surface and fold two pleats in the centre. Place butter side down on top of the pudding basin and secure with string around the rim. Before cutting the string, take it up over the top to create a loose handle, then tie securely. Trim off any excess foil.

Place the pudding basin on a trivet or an upturned saucer in a large saucepan and fill with enough boiling water to come two-thirds up the side of the basin. Cover, bring up to a simmer and cook for 2½ - 3 hours. Check the level of the water and top up with boiling water if necessary.

To serve, loosen the sides of the pudding with a knife and carefully turn out on to a plate.

Serve with custard or ice cream.

Banana Loaf

by Mandy Porter, *Teacher*, Giffnock, Glasgow

INGREDIENTS

170g self raising flour

Pinch of salt

340g of mashed bananas

112g of caster sugar

Quarter teaspoon of Bicarbonate of Soda

56g of butter or margarine

2 eggs beaten

85g chopped walnuts

METHOD

Preheat oven to 180°C.

Place all ingredients in a mixing bowl and beat well until light and fluffy.

Lightly grease a 2lb loaf tin.

Empty contents into tin and bake for 1 hour.

Brydies' Famous Tablet

by Isobel Brydie, *Lord Lieutenant*, East Calder, West Lothian

INGREDIENTS

1/3 pint of milk

1/2 lb margarine

2 lb caster sugar

397g tin condensed milk

METHOD

Dissolve margarine and milk on low heat in a large saucepan.

Take off the heat.

Add the sugar and leave for 30 minutes.

Heat for 20 minutes and bring to the boil. (Don't allow to boil until all sugar is dissolved).

Boil this for 20 minutes.

Take off the heat.

Add the condensed milk and stir then boil for 15-20 minutes, stirring all the time to prevent the bottom from burning.

Take off the heat and beat until thick.

Empty into a greased metal tray.

ACTION
DUCHENNE

Sponsors

Charles Macleod

COOK SCHOOL
BRAEHEAD FOODS

Notes

Notes